Moments of Magic
Shep Hyken

The Alan Press

MOMENTS OF MAGIC

A Shepard Presentation

The Alan Press
45 Colonial Hills Drive
St. Louis, MO 63141
(314) 692-2200
Email: shep@hyken.com
http://www.hyken.com

Library of Congress Catalog Number: 93-93567

ISBN: 0-963-78200-2

Printed in the United States of America
10 9 8 7

Acknowledgements

When it comes to writing a book, there are always so many people to thank...

There are so many speakers, trainers and authors that have influenced me. Thanks to the National Speakers Association for producing some excellent programming on various aspects of the publishing business.

Phil Wexler has been my friend and business associate. His ideas have been an inspiration to me over the years. His knowledge of the business has helped me tremendously.

Audrey Dietrich took the time to help "clean up" the book. She and her husband have been good friends and great supporters since the beginning of my professional career.

All of my clients had a place in this book. Whether they were mentioned by name or not, so much has come from my experiences with them.

Special thanks to Jim Braibish. His writing and editing abilities helped me to present my concepts in a readable and effective form.

On a personal level, there is my family. They have been encouraging. Six months ago I announced that I was actually going to start writing the book I had been talking about for over a year. Every day my wife, Cindy, kept asking, "Did you start yet?" For the last month she has been asking, "Are you finished yet?" Thanks for the enthusiasm.

Table of Contents

INTRODUCTION

How did *Moments of Magic* come to be?

The first speech I developed was a motivational speech titled, "You Are The Magic!" It mixed important messages with humor and magic. In 1987 I read one of the greatest books on service, Jan Carlzon's *Moments of Truth*. This moved me to turn my general motivational speech into a business presentation focused on the elements of outstanding service. This was during an era when most businesses were talking about customer service rather than providing customer service.

So the research began. I bought every book the bookstores had to offer in the areas of quality and service. At the time, I was working for many clients and had numerous opportunities to interview executives and experience how different companies viewed quality and service issues.

Then one day I was working with professional speaker and author Phil Wexler, who specializes in service and sales. Phil and I share very similar business philosophies, especially in the area of service. He told me of his concept of creating "Moments of Magic" (originating from Jan Carlzon's "Moments of Truth"). I told him how I also talked about Jan Carlzon's theories and how I used magic tricks to help back up the important points (the same way other speakers might tell stories or jokes). We knew we were speaking the same language.

It hit us both at the same time. I used magic in my speeches and Phil talked about magic in his. What a combination! The tie-in was perfect. Thanks to Phil, I had a new twist in my speech. As always, I would weave in the information, stories, and magic tricks, but I would add this one important phrase...

"Moments of Magic!"

This book is beneficial to everyone in any occupation in any business. The concepts are timeless and work whether you are the president, the secretary or the mail clerk. One of the important truths that businesses are becoming aware of, is that everyone is involved in service. You might be a bus driver or an assembly line worker. It doesn't matter. This book is for you.

The emphasis in this book is on relationship building and meeting expectations of the people you work with and sell to. And as an added bonus, much of this information will also work in your personal lives as well.

The goal of this book is to get you to think about quality service at all times. It is not a department or job description. It is an attitude. It is the way we have to do business.

"Houdini said: 'There is no trick getting the rabbit out of the hat; the real trick is getting him in there in the first place.' There is a similar law of life, that there is no trick getting success out of any of us; the real trick is getting within us the dedication, desire and perseverance that leads to success."

-- Cavett Robert

CHAPTER 1

THE MOMENT OF MAGIC

- How many times have you walked into a restaurant for a meal, and found the service and food so outstanding, that you left an extra-large tip and pledged to return again soon?

- Have you experienced repair people who fix your car or your house right the first time, at a fair price, and explain what they are doing, so that you would speak highly of them and recommend them to others?

- Have you been in the hospital and had nurses who seemed cheerful and caring, who did special things to lift your spirits toward a faster recovery?

- Have you stayed in hotels where all the staff seemed courteous and helpful, and truly made you feel like a VIP?

- Are there departments or people in your business on whom you can always depend for help, who promptly give you what you need and do so with a smile?

- When you talk to your boss, does he or she give you respect and encouragement?

All of these are examples of what I call *moments of magic*.

When you have been treated to a *moment of magic*, you feel extra satisfaction, knowing that someone has gone the extra mile to serve you. A *moment of magic* is receiving above-average service after you have become accustomed to average service. A *moment of magic* is getting something extra without paying for more. A *moment of magic* is a personal touch, knowing that someone cared enough to see that your work was done well.

No matter what business or occupation you are in, you can use the moments of magic concept to achieve greater success in your line of work.

When you create *moments of magic*, your customers will want to do business with you again and again. And, they will tell all their friends to do business with you.

We're In Business To Serve Our Customers

Let me ask you a question: What is the function of your business?

Most often when asked this question, people answer, "To make money."

But then I ask them to distinguish between the *function* and the *goal* of a business. Yes, the goal of a business is to make money, or in the case of a non-profit organization, to fulfill its mission.

The function of a business is what its people do in their jobs, day in and day out. Make money? Yes, ultimately.

But consider these important words from Dr. Theodore Levitt, senior professor at Harvard Business School:

The function of every business and organization is to get and keep customers.

No matter who you are or what you do, you have customers. You may call them patrons, buyers, clients, patients, tenants, volunteers, members, students, donors, faculty, staff, associates, partners, employees or any number of other names.

Whatever you call your customer, you have people whom you serve; people who buy your product or service... most often, with money.

Some customers buy the product by giving their time. These include members of churches, service clubs, and other volunteer organizations.

Employees, who are the internal customers, buy the product by giving their allegiance and hard work to the employer.

You depend on the customer for your living. You must understand your customer and what he or she wants.

Without customers, your business is dead. If you fail to satisfy your customer, they will walk away to the competition, or just not buy at all.

So, the most important task which your business faces each day, is *getting and keeping customers.*

Importance of Service

Good customer service is critical to business success in the 1990s. Ron Zemke, co-author of *Service America*, says 72 percent of our jobs and 68 percent of the Gross National Product are in the service sector. Tom Peters, author of *In Search of Excellence*, says General Motors is no longer considered a manufacturing company. Because of all the other businesses they are in, such as financing, data processing and automotive service, they are primarily a service company. In a Gallup Poll survey of 600 executives of Fortune 500 companies, the majority said that service will be the most important element to help them stay ahead of the competition in the 1990s. Most of the others felt that dealing with change would be the most important element. Perhaps they mean change in the way we deal with our customers and meet their changing expectations.

Internal Customers and External Customers

"I don't deal directly with the public, so my job doesn't involve customer service."

Wrong!

Every job in a company has an impact, directly or indirectly, on customer service.

There are two types of customers - *internal customers* and *external customers*. The external customer is the buyer of your company's product or service.

Within a company or organization, you also have many customers. Internal customers are the people in the next department with whom you work. An internal customer is the vice president for whom you do a special project, the employees in your department whom you want to build into a happy, productive team, the board of directors, and, of course, perhaps the most important customer of all... your boss.

In a business, many people depend on each other to get their jobs done. Accounting, sales and production all need each other. The secretary serves the boss by completing assigned responsibilities. The boss serves the secretary by providing a favorable working environment, constructive feedback and a commitment to helping him or her do the best job he or she can.

If you don't think you have customers, consider this: If you stopped doing your job for a week, who would notice?

Anyone who would notice is your customer. If no one notices, then your job is not having an impact on the company and the job probably should (and may) be eliminated.

In *Service America*, Ron Zemke and Karl Albrecht write,

> **If you're not serving the customer, you'd
> better be serving someone who is.**

In today's world, you're flirting with danger if you think that the customer service department is the only area involved in customer service. *Everyone* should be their own customer service department. Whether you are a clerk in the accounting department, or a sales rep on the floor, you have customers, and you are involved in customer service.

Meeting the Customer: The Moment of Truth

If the function of a business is to get and keep customers, how do we go about doing this?

Each time we meet a customer (internal or external) we have the opportunity to make or break our business.

Jan Carlzon, former president of Scandinavian Airlines, calls this the moment of truth. He says a moment of truth is:

> **"Any time a customer comes into con-
> tact with any aspect of your business,
> however remote, they have an opportu-
> nity to form an impression."**

He says there are a few main moments of truth at Scandinavian Airlines, such as ...

- At the curb when passengers pull up to check their bags;
- At the ticket counter when they purchase or confirm their tickets;
- When they board the plane;
- When they get off the plane; and
- At baggage claim area when they pick up their bags.

Then, there are many other moments of truth that happen in-between. You could be walking down the concourse toward the gate and pass a Scandinavian Airlines employee. If he or she smiles at you, that could be a positive moment of truth. If they frown at you, that could be a negative moment. These are very subtle moments of truth than can and do make a difference.

Carlzon says that in a year, each of the company's 10 million customers come into contact with approximately five Scandinavian Airlines employees. Thus, the company has 50 million moments of truth with its customers each year. Each of these contacts lasts an average of just fifteen-seconds.

Any moment of truth can go well or it can go poorly. When a moment of truth is great, I call it a *moment of magic*. A negative moment of truth is a *moment of misery*. Our job is to take all those moments of truth, and turn them into *moments of magic*.

Moments of truth can be big. But they are also the little things we do all day. For example, the way we answer the phone creates an impression. I might answer simply and abruptly, "This is Shep." Or, I could be more enthusiastic and say, "Good morning. This is Shep. How may I help you?"

Which way sounds better? Everything we do contributes to making *moments of magic*.

Moments of Misery

Sometimes all does not go well. Here are some examples of *moments of misery.*

You are driving to the grocery store. You notice a delivery truck pull behind the store, and they start to unload lettuce from it. You look at this delivery truck. It is the dirtiest, grimiest truck you have ever seen. If the outside of the truck is dirty, you must wonder what the inside looks like. You begin to have doubts about whether to buy lettuce or anything else from that store.

Or, you sit down in a restaurant. At your table, you notice dirt and pieces of food on the tablecloth, and dirt on the glassware. When the meal comes, you notice something on the plate that looks like it does not belong there. Would you want to finish that meal, or return to that restaurant?

Another *moment of misery* came when I visited a hospital lab for a blood test. Getting a blood test is not my favorite thing to do, and I especially do not like it when they prick your finger with a needle. My encounter with this hospital started in the admitting department. The lady in admitting asked me in a cold, terse voice, for my name, address, telephone number and all sorts of other information. I tried but could not get this lady to crack a smile. She was downright scary. It's too bad, because she is on the front line for the hospital. She is actually a public relations specialist for the hospital. But, unfortunately, she doesn't know it.

After finishing with the lady in admitting, I was almost ready to leave. It was such a negative experience, it actually scared me for the trip to the lab. Going to a hospital is usually not an enjoyable experience for most people. I am glad I was not really sick, or in an emergency. I would hate to have to deal with people like her during a time of pain. Those are examples of *moments of misery.*

Moment of Misery Becomes a Moment of Magic

One of my favorite service examples has to do with a cab driver I encountered while on a trip to Dallas. It was the middle of the summer, the temperature was about 99 degrees and the humidity was almost as high. It was hot. I walked out of the Dallas Convention Center looking for a cab. I carried two heavy bags on my way to the airport to catch a flight.

Up pulled this cab. The driver jumped out, and he was wearing cutoff jeans filled with holes. He had on a sleeveless shirt, with tattoos on his arms. He had not shaven for a week. His hair was a mess and his T-shirt had a radical joke written across the front.

Looking at this guy, I can tell you right now, that this was going to be a *moment of misery.* It was going to take 25 minutes to get to the airport, and I was going to have to ride with this guy for 25 minutes! Looking at him, I imagined how hot, smelly and dirty his cab was going to be.

Here was where the surprise began. In a mild mannered voice he said, "Sit down in the cab, it's nice and cool. I'll take care of your bags."

I did what he said and started to get inside the cab. When I opened the door, cool air hit me. The cab was spotless. In the middle of the cab there was a bucket with ice and two soft drinks. I looked down at the seat and there was a copy of *USA Today* and a local Dallas newspaper. Then I noticed he had a cellular telephone.

When he got in the cab, he said, "Have a soft drink. Use the phone if you need to make a call."

I asked him if this was his cab, or if he was borrowing it for the day. He assured me it was his cab. Then he offered me a piece of candy.

He asked where I was going, and I told him, to the airport. He flipped down the flag on the meter. I knew at that time in Dallas, the cabs had a flat rate from downtown to the airport. When he flipped down the meter, I thought he was trying to rip me off. I knew from experience that the meter is always higher than the flat rate. Then he said, "Sir, I'm flipping down the meter just to show you how much money you save with this flat rate."

My eyes lit up. This guy is much sharper than he looks. He's a salesman!

When we got on the highway, he asked another question. "Are you in a hurry or is it okay if I do the speed limit?"

"Just take your time," I said. As I drank his soda and read his newspaper, I wondered to myself just what kind of cab driver this was. I had never experienced a cab driver like this before.

We reached a certain point on the highway, and there was a fork in the road. Either direction would take us to the airport in about equal time. He said if we go to the right, it will take us through Las Colinas, where there is the most beautiful fountain. He asked, if I had a few minutes, could he take me to see it, and he would not charge extra since it was a flat rate. I humored him and agreed to go.

Soon we reached the fountain in Las Colinas. Yes, it was beautiful. It had huge, larger than life-size statues of horses (mustangs), running across the water. Where their hoofs hit the water, fountains sprayed up, as if the hoofs were splashing in the water. It really was the most beautiful fountain I had ever seen. You could see how proud he was.

We got back into the cab and headed back on our way to the airport. Now, he asked for my business card. He said he collects the business cards of the people he drives. I gave him my card and he gave me his. He said to call him the next time I am in Dallas. He would pick me up at the airport, even meet me at the gate. Limousine service at taxi cab rates. The fare was $22, but I paid $30 to give him a nice tip. It was a great ride. A *moment of magic.*

That's not all. As Paul Harvey would say, "And now, the rest of the story."

Four days later, I was in my office in St. Louis. I opened my mail, and found a thank-you note from my cab driver, Frank Nelson. I was overwhelmed and shocked. The note read, "I thank you for the opportunity to take you from the convention center to the airport. I hope you enjoyed the fountain..." That thank-you note made my day ... actually it made my week! How many times have you received a thank-you note from your cab driver?

Now, when I go to Dallas, I call Frank. Frank picks me up at the airport, and takes me anywhere I want to go. I have told others about him. While working a convention in Dallas, I gave his name to three of my clients. They used him... and he took everyone to see that fountain in Las Colinas.

Then, Christmas time came. What do I get in the mail from Frank Nelson? A Christmas card!

Frank Nelson treats his customers just the way he would want to be treated. His theory is that by doing this, he will make more money than any other cab driver in Dallas.

He is absolutely right! He does!

Magic... A Moment That Sparkles

There is a special reason I have chosen the term *moments of magic.*

Magic tricks are a classic way to dazzle an audience. Everyone enjoys a good magic trick. Magic has been an important part of my life.

I have been doing magic tricks since I was 10 years old. I found a book on card tricks and started practicing. By the time I was 12, I had learned many more tricks and started working birthday parties. At 14, I was doing magic tricks at night clubs in Aspen, Colorado.

While in college, I decided on a serious career in the oil business. That lasted until the company was sold, two and a half years later.

Since 1983, I have been speaking professionally and using magic tricks as a part of my speech. The tricks are an enjoyable way to help make an important point, the same way a speaker might tell a story or joke.

There are many parallels between doing a magic act and providing good customer service. When you stand up in front of an audience, you want to put a smile on people's faces. You want to do something they enjoy. You do the same thing when you reach the customer. You give them a good experience, a positive experience, a great experience. The audience wants more. The customer learns to expect the best.

Back in the days of working night clubs and banquets, I put a great deal of passion and enthusiasm into my magic show. That distinguished me from other magicians who had more raw ability and technical skill than I did. I was committed to doing a great job and giving the audience a good time. The passion showed through. While my ability was good, the passion and enthusiasm set me apart from the rest of the field. My job was to entertain, not just do magic tricks.

In business, it is the same. Everyone wants to take care of their customers, but some people care more and work harder at it than others. Good service can set a company ahead of competitors who have better products and less service. Showing that you care is of the utmost importance.

Going the extra mile in service creates magic for our customers, and makes them want to come back again and again. In entertainment, a *moment of magic* is when you leave the audience wanting more. In business...

A *moment of magic* is when you have done an exceptional job, when your customer is willing to do business with you again, and recommend you to others.

Third Try Is a Moment of Magic

My wife and I had the good fortune recently to buy a new home. That meant we had to sell our old home.

It took us a year and a half to sell the old one. We listed our home with two different agents, each of whom produced very little in the way of results. Over a year later we had little activity and no offers. It was a nice house in a good location; there was nothing wrong with it. It was just that the market was slow.

Things changed when we started working with Marilyn Singleton of Coldwell Banker. She was the fifth agent I interviewed.

When we met, she gave me a binder with all sorts of information. There was a letter from the president of Coldwell Banker, saying how great Marilyn was and how she was one of their top agents. The next page covered the listing agreement. Even though I had signed listing agreements twice previously, Marilyn explained it in greater detail. I learned things I didn't know before.

There was a clause she added to the listing agreement. It impressed me with just how much she believed in herself. Most listing agreements are for three or six months. Marilyn put in a clause that, if at any time I was not satisfied with her, I could cancel the listing, no questions asked.

Then there was the issue of price. Every agent told me I had to lower my price. The market was down, and sellers were taking less.

What set Marilyn apart from the others was that she gave me information to back up her recommendation. The others simply shared the opinion that lowering the price would make the home sell. That was it. She gave me a computer analysis of all comparable homes in my area that had been sold in the last year. She presented copies of information sheets on those homes, so we could compare them to mine, feature by feature. How many bedrooms? Finished basement? Fireplace? Updated kitchen and bathrooms? I had no problem lowering the price for her. Why? Because she gave me many good reasons to set the price where we did, backed up with solid information, not just an opinion.

Once I signed on with her, she continued to work hard. She made suggestions about sprucing up the house to make it more attractive. She offered to arrange for a lawn service and maids. She went to the house and supervised their work. Her lawn service was less expensive than the one I had been using! She or her assistant went to the house every other day, picking up newspapers, checking the mailbox, sprucing up and making sure the house was in tip-top shape.

Every week, she gave me a written report on all shoppers who visited the house, and what they liked and disliked about it.

Less than six weeks later, the house was sold. Marilyn Singleton had accomplished in six weeks what other agents could not achieve in over a year. She not only brought me one offer, she brought two offers at the same time. She started a bidding war for the house!

When it came time to close, I had already planned to be

on vacation. She knew I was going to be out of town, and arranged to have all the papers drawn up so I could pre-sign them before I left. She asked me for a deposit slip to my bank account, so the sale proceeds could be deposited directly into my account on the day of closing... while I was lying on a beach 2,000 miles away.

I have never experienced a level of professionalism and service as I have with Marilyn Singleton. Her attitude was, "I will take care of it, it's my job, I love what I do, I want you to be happy."

Isn't it great that somebody takes this much pride in his or her job?

Going the Extra Mile

I was giving a speech to staff members of Skywest Airlines, a commuter airline based in St. George, Utah. After my speech, the chairman of the board read the audience a letter he had received from a satisfied passenger. It was an outstanding example of a *moment of magic*.

The passenger was starting in San Francisco. He was going to take a connection to Los Angeles, and then fly to the Orient. Due to weather problems, the flight was delayed. The passenger was upset because he wanted to make his connection to the Orient flight. The Skywest agent phoned TWA, and asked if the passenger could get on TWA's Los Angeles flight. He was accepted and made a dash to the TWA gate. Once there, he found out the TWA flight was also delayed. So he dashed back to Skywest and took their flight. If everything went well, he would have just minutes to connect to the Orient flight.

Now, the Skywest agent could have stopped there and done nothing more. But he knew the Los Angeles airport, and knew the gate for the Orient flight would be on the other side of the airport from the Skywest gate. So the agent phoned Los Angeles and made arrangements for a Skywest representative to meet the passenger at the gate when he arrived. The Skywest representative in Los Angeles took the passenger in an electric cart to the Orient flight's gate. The Orient flight had been notified that this passenger would be arriving, but it would still be a very tight connection for him to make.

The passenger made the connection just in time, and was very grateful to Skywest for its help. By just making a few simple phone calls, the Skywest agent in San Francisco turned a moment of misery into a *moment of magic*.

> **Going the extra mile does not necessarily mean a lot of extra effort. It just requires caring and thinking about the needs of your customer.**

By the way, Skywest is bucking industry trends by receiving more positive letters than negative ones!

How You Can Make Magic

A magician isn't supposed to reveal how he does his tricks, but I would like to spend the rest of this book sharing with you insights into how to create *moments of magic* with your customers.

Start by bringing out the magic that is in you:
- Make a positive impression.
- Know your business.
- Be informed - know a little about everything.
- Show enthusiasm.
- Understand your customer.

Then, add these ingredients of a *moment of magic*:
- Provide quality.
- Respond quickly.

- Solve problems and answer needs.
- Be reliable.
- Say "thank you" and tell your customers they are important.

Remember, no matter who you are or what you do, you have customers. Your job and livelihood depend on satisfying the customer.

You are your own customer service department.

Whether your customers are high-powered executives, retail shoppers, the employees in the next department, or the people in your family, you can build their goodwill and trust... by making *moments of magic.*

Magic Hints

- The function of every business is to get and keep customers.

- There are two types of customers - external and internal. The external customer is the buyer of your product or service. Internal customers are the other people with whom you work in your organization.

- Whether or not you deal directly with the external customer, you are involved in customer service. Directly or indirectly, everyone serves the outside customer.

- Any time a customer comes into contact with any aspect of your business, that represents a moment of truth.

- A *moment of magic* is when you have gone the extra mile to give exceptional service to the customer. As a result, the customer does business with you again and recommends you to others.

"Always do right. This will surprise some people and astonish the rest."

-- Mark Twain

PART I
WHAT IT TAKES TO MAKE MAGIC

Giving outstanding customer service and creating *moments of magic* begins with you!

Before you meet your first customer, there are things you need to do to prepare. It is like having important visitors to your house for dinner. You think about the occasion and what will be happening at various times thoughout the evening. You get the table set and start to prepare the meal.

Creating magic does not come without effort. You must study and prepare. What you bring to each moment of truth with the customer, will have a significant impact on its outcome. Your attitude, appearance and knowledge are all important.

Good business people know how to present themselves, especially in selling situations. Any situation where we service the customer carries some degree of selling. We never stop selling ourselves and our businesses. We must always look for opportunities to highlight our positive attributes and build confidence with our customers. Every server, every bellhop, every cashier, every secretary, every consultant, every accountant, every executive, anyone who contacts the customer, has a moment of truth and a chance to sell the customer. When you sell the customer and gain their confidence and trust, you have created a *moment of magic.*

So, let's wave the magic wand, and find out how to harness your positive assets, and start making magic!

"Customers don't distinguish between you and the company you work for. To the customer's way of thinking, you are the company."

-- Ron Zemke
Author, Service America

CHAPTER 2

MAKE A POSITIVE
IMPRESSION

Someone once said you never get a second chance to make a first impression. In fact, the opposite is true. We never stop making first impressions.

Making a good impression yesterday does not mean you do not have to make a good impression today. It's like the old saying, "What have you done for me lately?"

Every time you are in front of your customer, you have an opportunity to make an impression. Every day, you have an opportunity to make a first impression. Remember, this applies not only to the outside customer, but also to your internal customer, your fellow employees.

The importance of first impressions is illustrated by this story from Bishop Fulton Sheen. He was visiting Philadelphia to give a sermon and decided to walk to the town hall rather than ride. He left the hotel and began walking. Soon he realized he was lost. He looked around and saw a couple of boys on a playground. He asked one of the boys to come over, and told him, "I think I am lost. Can you tell me how to get to the town hall?" The boy said, "Sure, that is easy." He gave directions, and the bishop thanked him.

The bishop asked, "Would you like to come and hear me

talk?"

The boy replied, "What are you going to talk about?"

The bishop said, "I am going to talk about how to get to heaven."

The boy stated, "I don't want to hear you talk," and the bishop asked him why.

The boy replied, "You can't figure out how to get to the town hall. I don't see how you can show me how to get to heaven."

The bishop obviously made a negative first impression. That first impression is very important. But even after you've made your first impression, you never stop making impressions. You must keep up the effort every day.

Be Up

When we meet our co-workers, customers, families and other people, we create a *first impression of the day*. If you walk into the office in the morning being cheerful and happy, people will reciprocate and they will treat you nicely. If you walk into the office crabby or withdrawn, you will turn people away. They will not want to talk to you.

It is especially important for supervisors to set an air of comfort. Employees need to feel comfortable going to the boss with a problem. Some supervisors carry such a gruff manner that their employees are terrified to bring up any issues.

When you pick up the telephone or greet your customer in person, even if it is the 100th time you've talked to that customer, you create a first impression of the day. You can change and influence your destiny every day in a positive direction or a negative direction. Always be upbeat. Create that *moment of magic*.

Sometimes we are going through difficult personal situations, like illnesses or family crises. It is difficult not to bring these problems to work. But, do not wear them on your shirtsleeves. Keep them to yourself. A professional work environment is not a place to air your personal problems.

In motivating yourself to give your best every day, keep in mind this verse:

I shall pass through this world but once.
Any good that I can do,
Or any kindness that I can show,
Let me not defer nor neglect it.
For I shall not pass this way again.

Dress and the First Impression

How you look and how you dress are very important. If you are an accountant or an attorney, do you wear the right type of suit? If you work in a restaurant, how do you look? Are your hands clean? Hair combed?

Dressing for success is important. Consider picking up a book on dressing for success. There are many to choose from at your local bookstores and libraries.

However, dressing for success does not always mean wearing a suit. It means dressing appropriately for the occasion. Dressing for success may mean one thing in the formal atmosphere of an executive board meeting, and it may mean something entirely different in my office which is casual. Often in my office, we are doing physical labor such as putting together manuals for a seminar. It would be silly to wear a business suit on those days.

When it is time to do a speech, it is time to dress for success. Then it is time to wear a good suit.

More important than just dressing for success is dressing appropriately. Once I was speaking to a group of installation managers for sprinkler systems. At their meeting, they were dressed casual. In that case, a sport-coat, open-collar shirt and a nice pair of slacks were absolutely proper. I knew this audience and I knew that to dress up would turn them off.

Another situation where appropriate meant something other than a coat and tie was an outdoor speech I did on a summer morning. The temperature was about 96 degrees. My speech was on teamwork, how people can work with one another, and do their part to contribute to each other's success. When I arrived at the site, I assessed the situation. I decided to wear my jacket when I was introduced, then immediately take it off. I wanted to make a good impression by wearing the jacket. I am a professional and I want to look the part. Then, I wanted to maintain some degree of comfort and show empathy with the heat my audience was also feeling.

Other Factors

How we maintain our workspaces makes a first impression. If you walk into an office that is piled with stacks of papers heaped on top of one another, how can you have confidence this person is going to be able to find information for you?

We form impressions every day among the people we serve and the people we work with. Part of the equation on how well we succeed depends on our attitude and our appearance.

Magic Hints

- Everyday we create an impression of ourselves with our customers. Remember, it is always important to present ourselves at our best.

- Be "up." When you are cheerful, people will reciprocate. Do not let outside problems affect you.

- Dress well. Dress appropriately for the occasion.

- Keep your office space attractive and well organized.

"All wish to possess knowledge, but few, comparatively speaking, are willing to pay the price."

-- Juvenal

CHAPTER 3

KNOW YOUR BUSINESS

If you want to interact effectively with your customers, you must know your business. You must know your product. You must be able to answer questions.

The more you know about your business, the more adept you will be at finding solutions to your customers' needs.

Eveready Battery maintains a close relationship with retail stores. The company positions itself as an expert in battery point of purchase. They offer to arrange a store's entire battery display and this includes the competitions' displays. They provide market information on what is selling and what is not.

More important, they act as a source of information on *all aspects* of the battery market. They are the "category manager." Retailers can go to Eveready with any questions about any aspect of batteries and how to set up their stores.

Pro Plan, a premium pet food brand marketed by the Pro-Vision division of Ralston Purina, provides similar expertise. They position themselves as experts in space management for the purposes of display and promotion of all pet food items. Pro-Vision also provides toll-free 800 telephone service for retailers and customers to call with general questions about pet foods.

My child's pediatrician offers a unique service to parents. He sets aside one hour a day, 8 to 9 a.m., to answer calls from parents. These are not medical emergencies like sick children, just general questions about care and prevention. His patients know this is always a time when he will be available to answer questions.

Become an Expert In Your Field

Knowledge of our businesses is vital. We never stop learning. We must continually read and study to keep abreast of new developments. When you become an expert in your field, you will gain the respect of your customers, both on the outside and within your organization. You will be looked upon as a source for information.

Why are consultants constantly writing articles and giving seminars? They want to share their expertise and position themselves as experts.

Present yourself as an expert and offer to be a source of information. Customers will come to respect you, and will be more likely to come to you for business.

Knowledge Helps Solve Customer Problems

If you know your business, you are better able to solve problems for your customers.

I made a phone call to a prospective client and talked about his needs and interests. He had a current need for a speaker, but I knew I was the wrong person for the job. Sometimes, it's hard to admit that to a client who is ready to sign a contract. But, instead of accepting a job that would have been wrong for the client, or saying, "No, I can't help you," I went a step further. I offered to find a speaker who would meet his needs. Part of the knowledge of my business is knowing my peers and their specialties. I gave the client three names, and one of them got the job. Did I give up a chance to get business? No. I presented myself as someone who is helpful and knowledgeable. Next time they need a speaker, it is likely they will consider me or at least ask for another referral. I will make myself available to them. I will follow up. I will keep trying, until I get the business for myself. Until that time, I will prove to be a valuable resource to them.

Know Your Product

You visit a fine restaurant. You study the menu and try to decide what to order. A good waiter or waitress will help you make your choice. They will explain how different items are prepared, and whether the food is spicy or mild. You can ask which items are best, and they will give recommendations.

Contrast this with the *moment of misery* I experienced when I asked a waitress which menu items she would recommend, and she replied, "I don't know. I just started working here."

One person who knows his business is my stockbroker, Jeff Silverstone of PaineWebber. I can call him anytime with questions about investments, and he will share his knowledge. I do not do all my investing business with him. Even if it is an investment I handle through another broker, I will still call Jeff for his opinion. He always is glad to help, and he gets most of my business.

Travel agents are another group to which product knowledge is important. Good travel agents differentiate themselves from average travel agents by the service they provide. Most agents can find you a low fare. But the best agents have up-to-date knowledge of all the fare programs offered by the airlines, cruise operators and others. They can suggest itineraries, give solid recommendations about hotels and find the best rental car.

Good salespeople must know their businesses. If you're going to buy a home or a car, you want to deal with people who can give you information. What features come with which price option? What are the estimated utility bills and fuel costs? What does the warranty cover?

Technical items such as computers are an area where most of us are vulnerable. We rely on the salesperson to explain the features of the various products, and help us select which one is right for us. Finding a good salesperson is especially important.

One salesperson who knows his business is John Bullock of Neiman Marcus, the upscale department store. John started out working in the gift department of Neiman Marcus. Out of his sheer interest in his work, he began studying about fine china. He went to the library and did research. He became familiar with the stories behind the major names in china such as Wedgwood. Now, customers go to him for information and advice on china.

Read Avidly

How can you become an expert? Noted speaker Brian Tracy says if you read on a subject for an hour each day, within two to three years you will become an expert. If you continue to read on this subject for an hour a day over three to five years, you will become an authority. After five to seven years, you will be an international authority. He adds, that if you read just one book a month, you will join the top one percent of the population.

I read every day on subjects related to my business, whether it be through books or magazines. My reading includes magazines about speaking techniques and about the subjects I cover, such as customer service. I attend the subjects I cover, such as customer service. I attend seminars and conventions for speakers. I keep abreast of my clients' industries, too.

To better myself in my abilities to get clients, I read a magazine called *Personal Selling Power* as well as numerous books on selling and client relations. I also read general publications such as *Communication Briefings, The Wall Street Journal, Bottom Line* and *Board Room Reports.*

Read every chance you get. If you have downtime while waiting at the airport, or waiting between appointments, that's a good time to read. Check out the nearest newsstand, or bookstore, or public library. Look for books and periodicals outside of your usual reading areas.

Read for fun, too. While most of my reading is business related, I do read fiction. Reading fiction stimulates the imaginative side of the brain, the right brain. It can help us be more creative in solving our everyday problems.

Harvard studies indicate that the key to self-motivation is perpetual growth. Unfortunately, studies also show that 58 percent of American college students never read a nonfiction book after graduation.

No time to read? Try cassette tapes. The average person spends 500 to 1,000 hours a year driving an automobile. What a resource of time to listen and learn! Many popular books, fiction and nonfiction, are available on cassette tape.

If you started now to use as learning time, those 500 to 1,000 hours in your car, in one year you would gain the learning equal to over one full semester of college.

Use On-Line Computer Services

I subscribe to the on-line service, Prodigy. I look through the headlines in it every day. The on-line services allow access to information on the various industries I work with. Using key words, like *oil* or *gasoline*, it will give me an up-to-date list of articles that have been written on the subject. This lets me know what is going on in the industry; the trends, problems and concerns. These services are a bargain. For a small fee, I have at my fingertips, more information than I can obtain at the public library.

Don't Fake It

I assigned an employee to watch a videotape. I asked her if she had watched it yet. She said "yes." I asked her opinion and she gave an evasive answer.

The next day she came into my office and said, "I feel like an idiot. I should have just told you I didn't watch the videotape."

I thanked her for her honesty. Knowing your business is great, but if the topic gets past what you know, don't try to fake it. Sooner or later, it will backfire on you.

Freshman members entering Congress in January 1993 were victoms of a prank that tested their knowledge of world events. A reporter from Spy magazine called 20 incoming congressmen and asked their opinions on "Do you think we're doing enough to stop ethnic cleansing in Freedonia?" Ethnic cleansing is a serious issue in the former Yugoslavian territory of Bosnia. However, Freedonia is a fictitious country from the Marx Brothers movie "Duck Soup."

All the congressmen fell for the prank. They gave answers like, "I think anything we can do to use the good offices of the U.S. government to assist stopping the killing over there, we should do."

None of the freshman congressmen thought to ask further about Freedonia and where it was. They gave answers that seemed to be politically correct, even though they had not heard of Freedonia.

Magic Hints

• Knowing your business makes you better able to help your customers.

• Become an expert in your field. Build a reputation as *the* person to call for information about your area of business.

• Know your product and all its features.

• Read avidly. Read professional magazines, business periodicals, and fiction. Attend seminars.

• Listen to audio cassettes in your car. The 500 to 1,000 hours you spend in your car each year, can equal one semester of college.

• Use on-line computer services to research your field and access timely information.

"If a man empties his purse into his head, no one can take it away from him. An investment in knowledge always pays the best interest."

-- Benjamin Franklin

CHAPTER 4

BE INFORMED -
KNOW A LITTLE ABOUT A
LOT

What if you were invited to have dinner this evening with the presidents of the five largest companies in America, or you found yourself sitting next to an interesting person on an airplane? Could you hold your own in conversation?

You can make a positive impression by demonstrating you are a well-rounded individual. Show that you have knowledge and interests not only in your specific field, but about the world as a whole. You don't have to be an expert. You just need to know enough to have some sense of what is going on.

General knowledge is knowing a little about a lot of things. It is knowing about world events and about the arts and sports. General knowledge is gained by reading the paper or watching the news. A great paper to read is *USA Today*. The articles are short and to the point. A great television program to watch is *60 Minutes* or one of the other good feature news shows. An interesting magazine that has great human interest stories is *People Magazine*. You will be surprised what you can pick up by just reading the front page of each section of your local paper.

If you learn a little about a lot of things, when you get

in front of your customers you can talk about things other than business. You can find out what their hobbies are and the things they like to do. Ask questions about what they do and discuss the answers. They will appreciate and respect your interest in them.

General knowledge helps to build rapport with customers. Aside from becoming an expert at what you do, you need to know what is going on in the world on a daily basis. If someone asks your opinion on a current issue, you should have something to say.

Not knowing about current events could make a negative impression. What if your customers are talking about a certain actor or hit movie that you don't know about, or even more important, a serious political issue? It could put you in an awkward situation.

In my profession as a speaker, it is expected that I have some knowledge of current events and trends. Other fields where this is important are marketing, advertising and public relations. For a barber or a bartender, the best reason to know current events is to be able to converse with customers. Even if you do not come into contact with the company's customers, you still work with people, your inside customers, every day.

Keep up with current events. You will build stronger and more interesting relationships with your customers and the people with whom you work.

Magic Hints

• General knowledge of the world shows you are a well-rounded individual.

• Learn a little about everything. Know enough about current events, art and sports to keep up a conversation.

• Knowledge contributes to building better relationships with your customers and people with whom you work.

"There is nothing as powerful and contagious as positive, uplifting enthusiasm that is handled wisely by a group of people who love one another and contribute their individual talents and abilities, coming together as one united force to reach one common cause, goal or dream."

-- Carl Mays

CHAPTER 5

BE ENTHUSIASTIC

If you are not excited about what you do or what you sell, how are you going to get the other person excited? Enthusiasm is contagious. If you are excited, it will cause other people to become excited. Enthusiastic people are fun to be around.

It can work the other way, too. If you are not excited, then they are not going to be excited either. Famous speaker Danny Cox says, "Enthusiasm is contagious. If what you have is lack of enthusiasm, that is also contagious."

Just one's tone of voice makes a big difference. Speaking in an energetic and enthusiastic tone of voice will spark enthusiasm in others.

Being excited about something lends credibility to what you do or sell. The person must really be involved in what is going on, and believe in what he or she is saying.

When we are alone in private, we can work extremely hard and be very serious. But when somebody walks into the office, or if we meet the public, we must show enthusiasm. If you have just finished a project, it might be appropriate to show some excitement and enthusiasm.

That could impact the results your project eventually achieves.

Give 100 Percent

All of us go through energy cycles. Sometimes we are enthusiastic. Sometimes we are flat.

The trick is to overcome those tired, lackluster times. Do not let your customer see any difference. Put your best foot forward every day, no matter what may have happened to you the night before.

I once did a program for a client when I was feeling absolutely miserable. I was sick. In fact, I was so sick that I was rushed to the hospital the night after with a 105-degree temperature.

Fortunately, in spite of being sick, I did get a good reaction to the speech. I put forth a 100 percent effort and didn't complain about the way I felt. Proof was that I booked four more engagements with the same client.

For another company, I had contracted to do a series of 12 speeches in a three-week period. On the last leg of this tour, I became ill. By now, I had become very comfortable with my speech material and I knew exactly what the audience wanted. I would stay in bed in my hotel room until it was almost time to go on. Then, I would wake myself up and take a real quick shower. I would go out there, put everything I had into that presentation, and five minutes after the speech, I was back in bed. Not one person in that audience ever knew I was sick.

Being enthusiastic means rising to the occasion and giving 100 percent of our effort.

Former professional racquetball player, Doug Cohen, knows what it means to give 100 percent. When he was on the pro tour he always gave 100 percent during the tournaments. And he also gave 100 percent at practice. On days when he woke up tired, he would still get up and play. At times when most players would quit practicing because of fatigue or boredom, he would continue at the same pace, if not harder. This type of practice paid off when he was tired in the middle of an important match. He had disciplined himself to continue his 100 percent effort even when he was down or tired.

This philosophy has carried over into Doug's career as a real estate professional. All of Doug's clients know and appreciate the effort and dedication he puts in for them.

Your customers will not accept "I don't feel good" as an excuse for poor service. Having a rough night, or not having a day off in a week, or having sick children, are not acceptable excuses for poor attitudes on the job.

Have a Positive Attitude

Maintaining a positive attitude is important to showing enthusiasm.

Do not let your problems drag you down. Avoid feeling sorry for yourself. Do not fuss over things you can't change.

Instead, look at your assets. Focus on what you can affect. Set goals and work to achieve them.

In your everyday life, find good things to say about yourself and others. Set out to make each day a great day. Live each moment for the best. Motivational speaker Dennis Waitley says, "Do we sing because we are happy? Or are we happy because we sing?"

No one likes to be around people who are always negative and complaining. There is a man at my health club who is a chronic whiner. He makes up names for people. Instead of calling me Shep, he whines, "Oh, Shepola." He never smiles. I've never seen him laugh. He doesn't seem to have any major problems in his life; he has nice family, even a dog. But I would never want to be around him. He would bring me down.

Problems create opportunities. Whenever anything negative has happened in my life, I have always said that there is a reason for this. Whenever I have an extremely negative thing happen to me, I realize that there are people out there who have it a lot worse. Children lose their parents, parents lose their children. Disease takes over someone's body. Compared to them, my problems are unimportant.

Even if you do not have control over the problem, the one thing you *always* have control over is your attitude. You can choose to make it a great day or a lousy day.

I once was driving around New Orleans with a client. We were looking for the restaurant where his customers were meeting us for dinner and ended up in a bad neighborhood. We were turning on this street and that street and had no idea where we were. The neighborhoods were getting worse.

Our tension and apprehension were building. My client was really starting to get upset. So I made a joke. I sarcastically said, "Oh boy, I'm going to die in New Orleans."

My client laughed. He then asked, "Okay, where are we?"

I said, "I know exactly where we are. We're right here. I don't know exactly where we're going, but we're making good time."

My client started to feel better. We made some levity out of the situation. And, obviously we did survive. We were a few minutes late to dinner. We could have been angry or upset about it, but our attitudes kept us in good spirits.

Low-Key People Can Be Enthusiastic

You do not always have to be an exciting, dynamic person to have enthusiasm. Everyone is different in how they express themselves. No matter who you are, you do have enthusiasm and can project it.

Your enthusiasm shows in the passion you have for your work. My business associate, Paul Wirtz, is an example of a low-key type of individual who still captivates you with his enthusiasm. We work together training people to become expense reduction consultants. Paul has been in this business for many years and knows the business inside and out.

When we present together, there is a big contrast between Paul and me. I am a very energetic and expressive speaker. Paul is an accountant by training. He has worked hard for many years. He is very laid back and somewhat detail oriented. His presentation style is completely opposite from mine. I joke about how when Paul was younger, he had a charisma bypass. Yet he keeps his audiences on the edge of their seats as much as I do. That is because he has a passion about what he does, and that passion shows through. He brings a dynamic energy from within, which has nothing to do with jumping around on a platform, getting people excited, or making people laugh. He does it through his credibility, through his desire to do a good job.

The president of a large corporation may be a terrible public speaker, but his employees and stockholders still respond positively to him. Why? Because he is knowledgeable and respected. If you believe in yourself and what you have, your credibility will show through. Your passion radiates energy and enthusiasm, even though it may not be physical energy, but mental energy.

Knowledge and Involvement Build Enthusiasm

Use your company's product, read about your subject and get involved in your field. That is one reason why an automobile sales person drives his or her demonstrator vehicle home.

If you sell home and personal care products, use them yourself. If you sell computers, read the personal computing magazines.

You also can build enthusiasm by getting involved in your profession. Join professional groups. Volunteer for committees and projects. Meet and talk with your peers.

Attending a workshop or meeting not only educates you, it can give you a fresh charge of energy.

Magic Hints

• Always show enthusiasm for what you do. Enthusiasm adds credibility.

• Give 100 percent - even when you feel lackluster.

• Have a positive attitude. See the positives in every situation. Don't fuss over things you cannot change.

• Low-key people show enthusiasm by their sincerity and passion.

• To build your enthusiasm, use your company's product, read about your subject and simply get involved.

"If we are not customer driven, our cars won't be either."

-- Donald Peterson
Former CEO, Ford Motor Company

CHAPTER 6

UNDERSTAND YOUR CUSTOMER

Who are your customers? What are their needs and wants?

Businesses spend millions on market research to learn about their customers. They study demographics and life-styles. They test-market products before investing in a full rollout.

As you work to build relationships with your customers, these are some of the most important words to remember:

Think like the buyer, not like the supplier.

A buzzword in many fields today is being market-driven. What that means is that an organization is developing its products or programs based on needs it has identified with its customers. That is thinking like the buyer.

The opposite of being market driven is being sales driven. A sales-driven organization says, "We have a warehouse full of widgets. We must find people to buy our widgets. Advertise, repackage, do whatever we have to do, but please, sell those widgets."

For years, companies have gotten away with that philosophy. But it will not work in the competitive market-place of the 1990s.

It has been said that in the 1950s and 1960s, Americans had lower expectations of products. When they bought new cars, they expected defects and tolerated them. They were not upset when windows wouldn't open or the car's tires were under-inflated. Then the Japanese came along with zero-defect cars. Americans now carry higher expectations of the cars and other products they buy. Our U.S. auto manufacturers are working hard to increase their quality.

Be Sensitive To Customer Needs

Put yourself in your customers' shoes. Consider how you would behave or react if you were in their situation.

Nintendo understands the people who buy their video games. They know that their customers, mostly young people, quickly master the games and become bored with them. They have a steady appetite for new games, but there also is a concern. If players get stuck or frustrated with the games, they may shelve their Nintendo sets and find other entertainment. So, Nintendo has a team of over 400 game counselors answering telephone inquiries from the company headquarters in Redmond, Washington.

Service hours are 4 a.m. to midnight, Pacific Time, Monday through Saturday, with shorter hours on Sunday. This is convenient to all time zones (when it's 4 a.m. in Seattle, it's 7 a.m. in New York) and to the evening times when kids are playing the games. How many 10 year olds would be allowed to make a long-distance call during business hours from school?

Nintendo says it has handled over 27 million calls since the center opened and now is servicing customers at the rate of over seven million calls a year. Nintendo says it spends $15 to $20 million a year on this telephone service center. That investment is worth every penny.

Kinko's Copies is a highly successful company structured around consumer needs. Its primary markets are self-employed people, homemakers and college students. Calling themselves "Your branch office," Kinko's strives to be a one-stop shop for all copying and document services. Open 24 hours a day, a typical Kinko's store has standard copiers, oversize copiers, color copiers, fax machines, and a bank of IBM and Macintosh computers available to customers. Sitting next to the copiers are supplies of scissors, tape, white out and other items a customer might need to make final adjustments in a document.

Butterball helps customers cook their turkeys through the Butterball Turkey Talk Hotline. Customers can call a toll-free 800 number for advice on how to cook a turkey. Butterball's research showed that many consumers feared cooking turkey because they did it infrequently. This toll-free service helps consumers overcome those fears... and helps Butterball sell more turkeys.

Ask Your Customers

Make an effort to find out what your customers' needs are. Solicit their comments.

Cavett Robert tells a story about a boy visiting a soda shop. He orders a root beer float and while it is being made, he goes over to the pay phone. The man behind the counter is listening in. The boy says, "Hello, Ma'am, I was calling to see if you need your grass cut today. Oh, you already have someone doing your grass? Does he edge around the sidewalk? Does he sweep up? Okay. So you're happy with the service? Thank you, anyway." He hangs up the phone.

The man behind the counter says, "I heard your conversation, and I'm sorry."

The boy asks, "Sorry about what?"

The man says, "It's obvious you didn't get the job."

The boy replies, "Oh, don't worry. There is nothing to be sorry about. I'm the one who already has the job. I was just calling to make sure I'm doing a good job."

This is what it takes. We have to stay in touch with our customers. We have to ask if they are happy, and what can we do to improve.

We want our customers to be demanding. We want them to bring their opinions to us. As long as they do that, and we do our jobs, the customer will keep coming back. When the competition gets fierce, they will stay with us regardless of price. They will stay when they know we are giving them something they cannot get anywhere else.

The importance of asking the customer was a lesson learned the hard way for a hotel and conference center on the West Coast. Looking to increase their convention business, they had produced a beautiful brochure filled with color pictures of all the center's amenities; golf, tennis, swimming and exercise facilities. The brochure was a huge failure. Why? Because the hotel did not ask the customers what they were looking for. The hotel did not think like the buyer.

The buyers of this hotel's convention services are meeting planners who schedule large, group events. From a meeting planner's standpoint, amenities like golf and tennis are a secondary priority. The planner has other concerns: How big are the meeting rooms? How are they configured? What audio-visual services are available? If those questions are answered satisfactorily, then the planner becomes interested in amenities.

Now, this hotel asks its customers about their needs, before they launch into expensive advertising campaigns. They hold focus groups and survey their customers. They do this in many areas of their business. One survey on coffee breaks produced an interesting result. Before the survey, the catering department predicted what seemed to be obvious: that coffee, tea and danish are the most important part of coffee breaks. They were wrong.

Do you know what the meeting planners considered the most important part of coffee breaks? Bathrooms. Meeting planners want to know how many bathrooms there are and how close they are to the meeting room. Executives in a meeting, after sitting for two or three hours, need to use the bathroom. They do not want to wait in line. Next priority is telephones. While on break, they want to call the office. There need to be enough telephones so the important executives do not have to wait to make their calls, and more importantly, are not late for the next meeting. Incidentally, coffee was at the *bottom* of the list, the least important part of a coffee break.

This is a good example of how it pays to think like the buyer, not like the supplier.

Formal surveys are just one way to find out what your customer is thinking. Small focus groups can give you great feedback. You can also use informal sampling techniques. Make a few calls to a random selection of prospects in the field. Or, ask questions and chat with your customers while you do other business. Some of my best feedback comes by sitting next to my clients on an airplane while returning from a speaking engagement.

One way that Anheuser-Busch finds out what its customers think is by sending their executives out into the field. The formal name for their program is "All Aboard." Executives will go out with delivery drivers in their trucks and ride to the various stops including grocery stores, liquor stores, restaurants and taverns. The executives will hear directly from retailers what their concerns are and what are those of their customers. The executives get a first-hand view of the market. That has to be one of the reasons Anheuser-Busch is number one.

Another good technique is comment cards. Wherever I go, I always fill out the comment cards.

Typically, a comment card will ask the customer to rate various aspects of the company's product or service. There is one question that is more effective than any other on a comment card. It should be the first one asked on the card. The question is:

What one thing can you think of that could have made this experience better?

If customers are mentioning the same issue over and over, then you know this is an area to which you need to pay attention. The beauty of this kind of survey is that it is open-ended and unprompted. You have not limited the customer's response by asking closed-ended or multiple choice questions. Problem areas can be brought to your attention.

Use Your Imagination

Once you have found out what your customers think and need, develop creative solutions to meet those needs.

Always ask, "How can we serve you better?" If more and more of your customers come from a certain area, perhaps you should open a branch office in that vicinity. If most of your customers are working people, perhaps you should establish evening hours. If you are in the office supply business, perhaps you could begin offering fax service since many of your customers are people who work out of their homes and may not own a fax machine.

In the movie "Big," Tom Hanks plays a boy who took the body of a young man in his 20s. He gets a job at a toy company. The owner of the toy company spots him playing with some of the toys. He offers some radical ideas for changing the toys which prove to be an immense success. That is because they came from the mind of a 10 year old who happens to be occupying an adult body. Hanks' best friend, still 10 years old, comes to visit him at the office and sees him playing with toys. "Don't you work?" he asks.

Hanks replies, "Working? I just play with these toys and tell them what I think. They pay me to play with toys!"

Creativity is seeing things from different directions. Professional speaker Joel Weldon says there are five ways to be creative:

Combination: Putting together two dissimilar items
Adaptation: Taking an idea from somewhere else and applying it
Substitution: Putting a different item in place of another
Minification: Making an object smaller
Magnification: Making an object larger

Joel uses the tape recorder as an example to illustrate this. Combination would be placing a tape recorder and radio in one unit. A child's toy tape recorder is adaptation. Substitution occurred when built-in microphones replaced separate hand-held mikes. Minification is the "Walkman" recorder; magnification is the "boom box."

There is a great book called *If It Ain't Broke, Break It* by Robert Kriegel and Louis Patler. Break-it thinking is a good approach. We need to keep questioning and challenging. "But we've always done it that way" is not an acceptable answer.

In the 1970s, Japanese carmakers began providing one key to fit both the ignition and doors of its cars. Although research shows customers prefer one key, some U.S. car companies are still providing two keys, 15 years after the single key was introduced.

We must constantly change the rules and assumptions we live by in the face of changing customer needs. Service is not just being nice and patting the customer on the back, it is giving them quality at every turn. It is giving them the product they want, and if it does not meet their needs, making it meet their needs. It means changing it as necessary. As the world progresses and people grow, they change. Giving excellent service encompasses meeting and anticipating the customer's expectations at every turn and understanding your customer.

Magic Hints

- Think like the buyer, not the supplier. Put yourself in your customer's shoes.

- Be sensitive to customer needs. Understand when and how customers use your product or service.

- Ask your customers for their opinions. Do formal surveys and use customer comment cards. Survey customers informally as you talk with them in person or by phone.

- The most important question on a customer comment card is, "Is there any one thing that we can do to serve you better?"

- Use your imagination to develop creative solutions to meet your customers' needs.

"Be our Guest,
Be our Guest,
Put our service to the test,
Tie your napkin round your neck,
We will do the rest...
...We live to serve"

PART II
WAYS TO CREATE MOMENTS OF MAGIC

You have decided to become a Magic Maker with your customers. You have polished your first impression and developed your knowledge about your business and the world around you. You are charged up and enthused, and you have learned all about your customers' needs and desires.

You want to stand out from the crowd, and do what it takes to get and keep that customer.

Customers today have high expectations. There is much competition. You cannot get away with delivering a shoddy product or poor service.

Following are five ways to set yourself apart with *moments of magic.*

"Quality is not an act, it is a habit."

-- Aristotle

CHAPTER 7

PROVIDE QUALITY AT EVERY TURN

Webster's defines quality as "excellence, superiority." Customers today want and demand quality. Shoddy products quickly gain poor reputations and fall by the wayside. Witness the Yugo automobile, which became the brunt of comedians' jokes because of poor reliability and eventually pulled out of the U.S. market. Yugo's failure also shows that customers do not make decisions on price alone. They will not buy a cheap product if it does not have acceptable quality.

Shoddy service leaves a company or organization with a poor reputation, also. If you go to a restaurant and have a bad experience, would you tell your friends not to go there? Would you return to a mechanic who does sloppy work on your car?

In today's marketplace, you need a good product *and* good service to succeed. That is what is called **providing quality at every turn**.

People expect a quality job and a quality product... quality in every aspect of what you do. Quality has become the buzzword, as Americans have been educated on issues of quality. Consumerism has taught the public about what

69

they can and should expect from business.

If nothing else, you must be aware of the quality of your competition. You must be at least as good as they are. You can't let the competition beat you on quality. As long as your quality is competitive, you can exceed your competition through good service.

No matter whether you deal directly with the outside customer, or your customers are your fellow employees, you need to give your best, and put quality into everything you do.

Lexus - An Example of Quality

Since their introduction in the U.S. market in the 1980s, Lexus automobiles have enjoyed phenomenal success. A new brand name created by Toyota to compete in the luxury market, Lexus has taken large numbers of customers from German luxury barons Mercedes and BMW, as well as the American stalwart Cadillac.

One reason why Lexus has been so successful is their complete dedication to quality at every turn. Here is part of the "Lexus Cares" mission statement:

"The challenge before Lexus is to create a new class of high performance and luxury in the automobile market. How will we do it? First we will offer a uniquely intelligent blend of functional technology, engineering and quality craftsmanship in our products. Then, we will complete the luxury experience by providing an unprecedented level of excellence in convenience and personalized attention in customer service."

Mercedes and BMW have reputations for outstanding engineering. Lexus holds its own with them in engineering. What really sets Lexus apart from its competition, though, is service.

Here is an example of how Lexus does things differently. Recently, they had to recall some of their vehicles. Usually, when there is a recall, a company will send computerized form letters to product owners, and put a notice in the news media.

Did Lexus issue their recall this way? No, because Lexus is not an ordinary car company. Instead, Lexus personally *telephoned* all the owners of affected Lexus cars. The representative asked when would be a convenient time for the dealer to *pick up* their Lexus from their home or business, and bring it in for the repair. While the Lexus was being repaired, the customer would receive another Lexus to use. *That* is service!

You won't find this kind of service from an ordinary company. Lexus' extraordinary attitude about service pervades every aspect of the operation. The following statement entitled "What Is Lexus?" is distributed to the company's dealers and sales force:

"Lexus is... Engineering sophistication and manufacturing quality.

Lexus is... Luxury and performance.

Lexus is... An image and expectation of excellence.

Lexus is... Valuing the customer as an important individual.

Lexus is... Treating customers the way THEY want to be treated.

Lexus is... A total experience that reflects professionalism and a sincere commitment to satisfaction.

Lexus is... Doing it right the first time.

Lexus is... Caring on a personal level.

Lexus is... Exceeding customer expectations.

And... In the eyes of the customer, I AM LEXUS !!!"

Quality Is Something That Lasts

Quality service means nothing if the product keeps breaking and has to be repaired constantly.

The ads with the lonely Maytag repairman tell us that a Maytag is built to last, and will seldom be down for repair.

A telephone equipment company once found out what problems poor materials can create. They had outstanding service people. Their phones and switching equipment were well-made. However, they compromised on wiring and other peripheral materials.

The service people had to keep going back for repeat service calls to the same customers. No matter how good the service people were, the system was going to keep breaking. Trained people and a good service philosophy could not make up for poor materials.

Lasting quality applies to more than just automobiles, appliances and other mechanical devices. Those serving internal customers have important quality considerations. Perhaps you have been asked to write a report. Delivering quality is doing a thorough job and making sure the report truly reflects the situation as you know it. The quality report tells the information needed to make a sound decision.

Those who skimp on quality may do the minimum and

"tell them what they want to hear." Others may supply volumes of meaningless information just to give the impression of thoroughness.

For a consultant, quality is asking the tough questions and delving into the deeper issues with a client. Builders and architects achieve quality when they design buildings that meet all foreseeable needs of the people who will use the building. Quality building design also is setting standards and tolerances to withstand major earthquakes and other extreme circumstances.

Quality Is Cleanliness

One day many years ago, Walt Disney took his young daughter to an amusement park. The roller coaster was rickety, and the place generally was dirty.

"How could anyone take a child here?" he asked. "One day, I want to create a theme park where families can enjoy themselves, and know it is safe to go there."

So Disney bought a plot of orange groves in Anaheim, California. The rest is history. Today, Disney theme parks set a quality standard for the rest of the industry. They are meticulously clean, and personnel are always friendly and hospitable.

Disney theme parks show how cleanliness is part of quality.

If you take your car to a repair shop and find the shop filled with grease and a mess of parts and tools, doesn't it make you wonder what they will do with your car? It's an unwritten rule that a good measure of a repair shop is its cleanliness.

Another way to show cleanliness and quality is in your written materials. Quality is cleanly typed correspondence, and clean, attractive literature. It is words spelled correctly and sentences well written. If you receive a piece of sales literature that looks like the 12th generation of pieces assembled on a photocopier, doesn't it make you wonder about the professionalism of the people behind it? With all the capabilities of modern word processing systems, including spell checkers, type fonts and laser printing, there's no excuse for messy correspondence. The newest systems even have grammar check!

Quality Is Value

When we spend our money, we want to feel we are getting our money's worth.

If I spend $12,000 on a Saturn, I expect a reliable, economical, reasonably comfortable car. If I spend $30,000 for a Lexus, I expect all of this at a much higher level. For the price of the Lexus, I am much more picky about ride, handling, and amenities like the stereo system. And, I expect each car to be at least as good as the competition in its class.

For dinner, I can go to an exclusive Italian restaurant in the famed Hill section of St. Louis, and have a chicken parmesan dinner for around $50 a person, including drinks and tip. Or, I can get chicken parmesan at a chain restaurant, and pay $10 a person. At the expensive restaurant, I expect a high degree of refinement in the cooking, the service and the atmosphere. At the chain restaurant, I expect a good tasting meal in a pleasant atmosphere. In either case, I expect something in line with what I am paying.

Years ago, Toyota differentiated themselves from other cars on the basis of quality. They said their doors would slam just as quietly as those on luxury cars. The implication was you could get the same level of quality from a Toyota for much less money than a luxury car.

There is a famous delicatessen in New York City called

Carnegie's. You will pay twice as much for a sandwich there than you would at most delicatessens around the country. What do you receive for it? One, the unique experience of the place, with the waiters' "Don't give me no trouble" attitude. And, two, their sandwiches are so thick that you probably won't finish them. They are always filling! You will never leave hungry. It is an experience. You get a lot for your money.

Quality Is Information

You can enhance the quality of your product or service by giving information to your customer. People like to know about you and your product. Everyone may not be interested, but for some, information can be a *Moment of Magic*.

When you take something to be repaired, it always helps when the service person explains what the problem is, and why it occurred.

If you are having a home built, it is nice to know the grade of the lumber and how far apart the wall studs are being placed. It may be interesting to receive information about the history of the property and the area on which your home is being built.

Information can be given one-on-one by sales or service people, or it can be disseminated through brochures and other written information.

Many national associations in the health-care field publish pamphlets for use in doctors' and dentists' offices. Subjects range from orthodontic care to orthopedics.

On the side of every can of Budweiser beer, the label explains the Beechwood Aging process used to brew the beer. Some businesses, such as consultants and hospitals, publish newsletters for their customers and prospects.

For internal customers, you can regularly prepare reports about your work, and circulate these to other key people. Also, try to present your report in person, rather than just toss it in someone's in-basket.

Lack of information can be a negative. Have you ever bought something, and then couldn't use it because you could not understand the directions? It went on the shelf. Computer software and video games are notorious for poor or incomplete directions.

One software package with detailed directions is WordPerfect. It comes with a huge reference manual, organized alphabetically by subject. Want to learn how to set margins? Just look under "m."

Information is a tool you can use to sell your customers on you and your product, and reinforce the sale again and again.

Magic Hints

• People expect quality.

• Study your competition and make sure you are at least
  equal on quality. Beat them with superior service.

• Give lasting value. Provide a durable product. Do it
  right the first time, every time.

• Quality is cleanliness. Keep your facilities clean. Make
  your people look good. Make correspondence neat,
  clean and attractive.

• Give customers their money's worth and more.
  Do not skimp. Be like the restaurant that gives generous
  portions.

• Provide information. Explain the product and how it is
  made. Let the customer know what you do, how you do
  it and why you do it. Provide status reports and project
  updates.

"Of course I want it today. If I wanted it tomorrow, I would have given it to you tomorrow."

-- **The Boss**

CHAPTER 8

RESPOND QUICKLY

We live in the electronic age. On our TV sets, we can watch wars being fought halfway around the world. Within seconds, we can fax business papers to Japan.

You can walk into a grocery store, pick up a couple items, walk over to the cashier, and they scan the items across a little electric eye. You hear a beep, and a moment later, they tell you how much you owe.

We are conditioned for quick response. What used to take minutes or days to calculate, now can be done in a matter of seconds, if not instantaneously.

So when it comes to people, customers expect the same quick response they are used to getting from electronic equipment and technology.

More than ever, it is imperative that we handle customer requests on a timely basis. Quick response is important. The speed at which you take care of a customer will greatly enhance the chances of the customer coming back to you again. For internal customers, the speed at which you respond will enhance the confidence that fellow employees have in you to get things done.

One of the things that differentiates some successful

people is how fast they work with the client. Some people take months to get information back to the client, while others can literally do it in days. Ironically, they are giving the same information! If you come back right away, the client is still excited about the project. If you wait months, you could face a response like, "Oh, you're back. I wondered if you ever were coming back."

If someone inquired about my business and I did not respond quickly, chances are that client would move on to someone else who did respond quickly.

Once, I almost lost a prospective client because of a lost telephone message. The client called on a Monday morning and said they needed a speaker, it was the second time they called, was I interested? I did not know about the previous call on Friday, because the message had not been given to me. I asked when they needed the speaker. They said next week. I reacted quickly. Since the client was located in St. Louis, I was able to send my information packet by courier. The client had the material within an hour. That same day, the client received in the mail, material from two other speakers. Fortunately, I got the job.

No doubt, my quick response that Monday morning gained me an edge with this client.

Here is a basic rule to follow when it comes to timeliness:

Don't keep the customer waiting.

Depending on what you do, the length of time required to respond will be different. If you have a request to send a piece of literature, it can be put in that day's mail. If you must do some research or prepare a report, it could take longer.

Telephone calls always should be returned the same day. An even better goal is within an hour or two. Thanks to pagers, cellular phones, voice mail, remote-access answering machines and other technologies, you always can stay in touch with your calls.

Whatever you do, avoid the mentality of some company executives who never return phone calls or answer memos. You have to call them five times to get an answer on something. And, avoid the attitude of some organizations which publicly announce they need four to six weeks to process simple requests for literature.

Ask When They Want It

Some things really need to be done right away, and some don't.

Start by asking your customer *when* they need what they are requesting. This is especially true for internal customers.

You have to understand people's language. "As soon as possible" may mean today for your boss. It may mean within the month to someone else.

Find out what the response time needs to be. If you are given an unrealistic time frame to respond, then tell the person what they can expect from you, and by when. There may be time needed to do the research, or build the sample products, or do the artwork.

If you cannot respond immediately with a full answer, you can start by simply acknowledging the request. Write a letter or memo back saying, "We received your request. It will take 'x-time' to process." Then, explain why it will take more time.

Another technique is to provide interim reports or executive summaries. Perhaps you have just done a survey. You've tabulated the data and you know what the findings are, but you have not put together the full report. Your executive has an important meeting tomorrow, and there is not time to finish the final report. What you can do is prepare a memo to the executive summarizing "preliminary findings."

Here is another example. A consultant has been brought in to study a certain area of the client's business. The client is anxious to hear the results of the study. The consultant could say, "I cannot give you full information now, since there is much research to do. However, I will give you weekly updates. This is where I am now and this is the next step. This is when it will be finished."

The client normally will be understanding, provided there are legitimate reasons. You cannot just say, "I didn't get around to it." Delays can and do occur. Those are acceptable, but procrastination is not.

You should bring a sense of urgency to all your dealings with the client. Do not put off until tomorrow what can be done today. Do not keep the customer waiting. Provide a time frame and stick to it.

Magic Hints

- In this electronic age, rapid response is the norm.

- The speed at which you take care of a customer will greatly enhance the chances of the customer coming back again.

- Do not keep the customer waiting.

- Return phone calls and answer letters promptly.

- Ask when the customer needs what they are requesting.

- If you cannot fulfill the request immediately, acknowledge the request and provide a timetable. Give status reports.

"Use your own best judgement at all times."

--The entire policy manual of
Nordstroms

CHAPTER 9

SOLVE THEIR PROBLEMS

Solving problems is the direct action phase of *moments of magic*. This is where you go to work for the customer. You will have the chance to harness your creative talents to find "win-win" solutions to the stickiest of situations.

We face a wide variety of problems. Sometimes, it may be something as simple as "I've moved, please update my address." Or, you may be an attorney who has been asked to negotiate a complex series of deals to protect a client's interest.

Some problems are immediate, like a car that will not start. You can also look at problems in a long-term view. You may look beyond the immediate situation, and think more deeply about the needs of the customer. A local bank was hearing more and more of its customers say they work during the day. They cannot get to the bank when it is open. The bank's response was to extend its hours into the evening.

Fix the Problem

When the customer gives you a problem, make sure you solve it. The worst thing that can happen is for the customer to have to come back again to get something fixed. That's a big turnoff.

The bottom line is this:

> **You can be knowledgeable and enthusiastic and respond quickly, but if you do not fix the problem, you will not satisfy the customer.**

Here are three steps to help put you on track toward solving problems.

Listen to your customer. Hear the whole story. Don't jump to the conclusion that this is just like another situation you have handled. Ask clarifying questions.

Understand the situation. Think about the implications. Put yourself in the customer's shoes. Analyze the root of the problem. Ask appropriate questions to make sure you have a complete understanding of the situation.

Respond with an effective solution. Develop a solution that will meet your organization's requirements and satisfy the customer's need.

Finding Solutions

Xtra Leasing, a trailer leasing company in St. Louis, had leased hundreds of trailers to a particular customer. Somehow a defect was spotted in some of the new trailers. The lugnuts on the wheels would loosen and fall off. Then the actual wheels would come off while the truck was in motion, creating a very dangerous situation. After some research, it was determined that the problem was not the fault of the leasing company, but of the manufacturer.

The leasing company went to the manufacturer with the problem. After looking into the situation, the manufacturer admitted the problem, but said only 10 percent of the wheels were bad, and that is all they would take care of. However, the leasing company had a better appreciation of its obligation to the customer. It replaced *all* of the wheels on the vehicles for this client. The leasing company took more responsibility than the manufacturer would. They went above and beyond the call of duty. Taking responsibility for this problem cost Xtra a lot of money in the short term. But in the long term, the customer's renewed confidence was overwhelming. It helped to solidify the relationship with the customer. Xtra turned a *moment of misery* into a *moment of magic.*

Another company that solved a huge, potentially catastrophic problem (which was not its fault) was Johnson & Johnson, with the Tylenol scare in 1983. Someone had broken open Tylenol packages and laced the capsules with cyanide. Johnson & Johnson immediately pulled all Tylenol from store shelves nationwide. In the short run, it cost them dearly. In the long run, it paid big dividends. Trust is essential to anyone in the pharmaceutical business; people are not going to take a medication they can't trust. Johnson & Johnson increased the confidence of the public by acting thoroughly and decisively and in the interest of their customers.

Creative Solutions

Recently I became interested in one of the new four-wheel-drive sport-utility vehicles on the market. I had made several trips to the showroom to admire its sturdy, outdoors appeal. The model I wanted carried a price tag of over $30,000, putting it in the same range as many luxury cars.

When I began serious negotiations with the salesman, we ran into a snag. One thing I really wanted was a free loaner car anytime mine goes in for major service. I was aware that a number of other automobile dealerships offered their customers this arrangement. I asked the sport-utility vehicle dealer if he could give me a free loaner while my car was being serviced. He said, "No, we don't do that. It's not our policy." I told him his competition was willing to do this. He asked who I was referring to. I told him about three other automobile dealers' service policies. He said the other cars were more expensive. They could afford to give the loaner. I told him he should check out his competition. Two of the dealers had cars starting in the mid-to-high teens.

A possible solution for this sales person would have been to raise the price offered on the sport-utility vehicle to cover any rental costs. I would have paid more to have a service I consider important. Because the dealer couldn't be flexible enough to find a creative solution, he lost my business.

Recently my wife and I had our kitchen remodeled. The contractor made two mistakes, both of which were corrected effectively.

First, he installed the wrong kind of formica. We had specified a certain grade of formica for the counter tops, called ColorCore. Standard formica has a brown edge, covered with a color laminate. ColorCore is the same color all the way through, with no brown edge. The contractor accidentally ordered standard formica. After realizing his mistake, he offered to sell us the standard formica for a substantial discount. However, because our counter tops were light gray, the brown core detracted from the appearance, and my wife insisted we go with ColorCore. The contractor admitted his mistake, and absorbed the cost of replacing the formica without hesitation.

Our contractor's second mistake occurred in building a

space for our refrigerator. He measured the space to fit a certain high-end type of refrigerator called Sub-Zero. It takes up less space because the condenser is on the top instead of the back. When we tried to move in our standard refrigerator, guess what happened? It didn't fit. We faced a *moment of misery*. He would have to rip apart half of the kitchen to fix this problem. What did he do? He found a creative solution. He sold us a Sub-Zero refrigerator at a discount. He avoided having to redo the kitchen, and we got the high-end refrigerator we had eventually hoped to buy anyway at a very good price. Everyone was happy.

Employers can find creative solutions to the special needs of employees. Consider the case of a single mother with young children. She wants to leave work early to take care of her children after school. Perhaps the employer can allow her to adjust her schedule with flexible hours, making up time on Saturday. Or, arrangements could be made for her to do some of her work at home after her children have gone to bed. Many companies are doing this. They call it "Flex Time."

Recognize Problems

Sometimes your customers don't tell you about a problem. You just have to recognize that there is one. A simple concept of prepared meals solved the problem for consumers of a major grocery store chain. The company's executives realized that there are more and more double income families. The tradition of one "bread earner" and one home-maker is changing. The problem was who would make dinner if no one stayed home?

Convenience was the solution to the problem. The company hired chefs to work at each store to prepare ready-to-eat meals that were healthy and nutritious, but most of all, good. Their meals ranged from individual portions to large roasted chickens. All the customer had to do was pick up the meal on the way home from work and reheat it when they were ready to eat.

Someone once said, "Problems create opportunities." Perhaps a better more positive word for "problem" is "situation." Analyze the "situation" and deal with it. Turn the "situation" around and make it an opportunity to show how good you and your company are.

In most cases, if you do business with a customer long enough, you will eventually have a "situation" happen. It is how you handle this situation that will keep the customer coming back. Let them know they can count on you. And when a moment of misery happens, they know that you will make it right, and turn it into a *moment of magic*.

Magic Hints

• No matter how knowledgeable and enthusiastic you are, if you do not solve the problem you will not satisfy the customer.

• Listen carefully to what the customer says. Make sure you understand the situation before you take action.

• Respond quickly, decisively and thoroughly, so you can maintain the customer's confidence.

• Use creative problem solving to find "win-win" solutions. Be flexible. Do not be limited by policy or past practice. Be willing to bend the rules as long as it does not hurt the business.

"This is the earliest I have ever been late."

-- Yogi Berra to Joe Garagiola

CHAPTER 10

BE RELIABLE

Mark Twain said, "The only things you can rely on are death and taxes."

Indeed, sometimes it may seem like there are very few people or institutions we can rely on. Sometimes the problem just does not get fixed, or it takes repeated phone calls to get an answer.

That is why it is all the more important for you to prove to be reliable in how you handle your customers' questions, problems and complaints.

Reliability is the appliance service man who was scheduled to come to my house the day a heavy snow was forecast. He called the day before to let us know that he would try to keep his appointment with us in spite of the snow.

Reliability is the hotel where I can stay, and always receive a good room and excellent service. If and when problems arise, they have proven that they will take care of them.

Reliability is the fellow employee you can call upon for information or help, and you can count on them to have the material to you within a short time that afternoon, the next day or whenever promised.

Being reliable starts with your attitude. Reliable people do "whatever it takes" to get the job done. If they must stay 30 minutes late, or work through lunch, they do it. If they have to rearrange priorities, they do it. They make the extra effort. They view their jobs not in the clock-puncher mentality of "I can't wait until the day is over," but instead, "I enjoy what I am doing, and I'm going to have a great day helping people." They do what they do because they want to, not because they have to.

Dennis Waitley attacks those who carry the "Thank God it's Friday" attitude. He suggests we say instead, "Thank God it's Monday," and focus on all the positive things we are going to accomplish with our week.

Zig Ziglar tells a story about a group of men working in a railroad yard. A limousine drove up and a well dressed man got out. He walked over to one of the workers and said, "Hi, Charlie, how are you doin'?" They exchanged pleasantries, then the man got back in his limousine and drove away. The worker's colleagues asked what that was about. The worker said, "That's my friend Bob. He is president of the railroad. We started here at the same time, 25 years ago."

A co-worker asked, "How come he's president of the railroad, and you're working here in the yard?"

The worker answered, "Twenty five years ago when we started here together, I went to work for a paycheck. He went to work for the railroad."

That is the attitude of dedication we must take. The worker was reliable in that he showed up for work every day. But the president did much more. He immersed himself in the business.

Reliability can be summed up by asking yourself this question:

How easy and desirable are we to do business with?

If someone is easy and desirable to do business with, you know they will always accommodate your needs. They are accessible. They are flexible, accountable and always follow through.

Here are tips on how you can become more reliable:

Be Accessible

That is the first requirement for being easy to do business with. If people cannot find you, they cannot bring their demands or needs to you.

For a business, this means having hours that suit your customers. It may mean toll-free 800 telephone service, perhaps with operators on duty in the evenings and on weekends. It means having enough service people on the floor to handle the volume of customers at peak times. It also could mean having various locations around town, so people do not have to drive far to do business with you. It could mean taking your program or service to the customer's location, such as the way Red Cross teaches first-aid or CPR classes in workplaces.

For employees, accessibility is critical. Avoid unnecessary absences from your office, so people can find you if they need you. When you are out of the office or on the phone, have a secretary or voice mail take your messages. Return phone calls as soon as possible. Do not prolong meetings. Consider an "open-door" policy.

If you are on a hot project, give key people your home telephone number. When you travel or leave the office, provide a number where you can be reached.

One tip on reliability in your personal life. If you do not

have a telephone answering system, get one. That way, people will not have to keep trying to call you over and over. Busy people sometimes exchange messages via answering machines and voice mail, without talking to each other. One valuable feature of most newer machines and systems, is that you can dial up your messages from a remote location. So, you can be absent all day, and still keep up with your messages.

Be Flexible

Do what it takes to get the job done. Avoid the attitude of, "We've never done it that way before," or "That's not policy."

If your customer needs something right away, courier or fax it. If they need it the next day, send it by overnight express.

Accommodate reasonable requests. If the customer asks you to have their meal ready at noon for pickup, do it. If they want a club sandwich without bacon, leave off the bacon.

In the 1970 movie "Five Easy Pieces," Jack Nicholson walks into a diner and asks for whole wheat toast. The waitress says, "We don't serve whole wheat toast." Nicholson says, "I know you have whole wheat toast, because you serve a chicken sandwich on whole wheat." She continues to refuse, so he asks for a chicken sandwich, but hold the chicken, lettuce and mayonnaise. He pays for the chicken sandwich just so he can get his whole wheat toast.

Several years ago, I was buying a home. Even though I could afford it, I was having great difficulty getting a loan since I was self-employed. Bankers were scrutinizing my business income and my business plan. One day, I read a commentary by Mark Vittert in the *St. Louis Business*

Journal about how people don't do business "on a hand-shake" any more. The article was about a time when integrity and trust were major parts of doing business, and people did not rely just on information off of a form. That same day, I ran into a banker named Hord Hardin. I explained my situation, and he listened. We made an appointment to talk about the loan. I filled out the forms, showed him my tax returns for the last two years, and presented my speaking engagement calendar. The bank gave me the loan on the spot. There was never a late payment, and the loan was paid off early. Hord Hardin was willing to have a little faith in me, and do business "on a handshake."

Follow Through

Robert Schuller says, "Those who fail, fail to follow through." If you say you are going to do something, do it. If you say you will mail the information, then mail it. If you say you will have the project done by Monday, get it done. Or if there is a good reason it is not done, let your customer know what is going on.

Sometimes, sales people are not good at following through. They are good at building excitement, but not at the knitty gritty work. Follow-through often is a series of basic tasks.

Keeping promises to our customers is essential to building trust.

One person who follows through for me is the man who sold me my car, Harl White. While making the deal, he was always reliable and dependable. Whenever I needed service, he has arranged for a loaner. One time, I had my car in for service, and was given a compact car as a loaner. That would have been fine, except that I was picking up three clients at the airport later that morning. I needed something a little bit larger. I presented the problem to Harl, and he loaned me his demonstrator, a brand new top-of-the-line Mercedes. He certainly impressed me, and I certainly impressed my clients!

Be Accountable
   If something goes wrong, stand up and face the situation. Take responsibility.
   The staff of the Ritz-Carlton hotels provide a wonderful example of accountability. One of the rules of the Ritz-Carlton is, that whenever a customer presents a problem ("opportunity" in Ritz-Carlton language) to an employee, it is that employee's responsibility to see that the "opportunity" is resolved.
   If a customer wants directions to the banquet room, the employee will walk the person there, rather than just give directions. If a customer goes to a bellman and says a light in the room is broken, it is the bellman's responsibility to get the light fixed. The bellman may need to call maintenance or housekeeping to have them do the actual work, but the bellman will follow through to see the work is done. The bellman will then contact the customer to make sure the problem has been resolved to his or her satisfaction. In other words, the bellman owns the problem.
   Here is another example of how the Ritz-Carlton gives extraordinary service. A customer arrived in town late one night. He did not have a reservation at the Ritz, and the hotel was full. The clerk at the desk checked another hotel two blocks away. It had a room, so the Ritz booked the man there. The bellman then drove the man and his luggage to the second hotel. But that's not the end.
   It was midnight, and the man was hungry. The bellman knew this. He also knew that the second hotel's restaurant and room service had closed for the night. So he ordered

a meal from the Ritz's room service. The Ritz's room service delivered the meal to him - two blocks away. Needless to say, he spent the next few nights at the Ritz. The Ritz did not have to take care of this customer, since he had not guaranteed a room for late arrival. But the Ritz took control of the situation and turned it into an opportunity to win the customer's confidence. They demonstrated 100 percent accountability.

Neiman Marcus is another company which empowers its employees with a wide range of accountability. A Neiman Marcus employee does not just work in one department. They are able to sell in all departments.

One of their very best employees works in the St. Louis store. His name is John Bullock. In an earlier chapter, John was noted as an example of someone who knows his business.

John also is a good example of someone who is very reliable and accountable. You can depend on him to follow through. When I got married, I was looking for a gift for the groomsmen. I found a leather address book at the Neiman Marcus store where John was working. The problem was, they only had one book. John said he would make sure I had these gifts, and not to worry. He called to other stores around the country; he had to go to six stores to get the seven books I needed.

Today, when the St. Louis Neiman Marcus store trains new employees, John Bullock is presented in the training session as an example of what a good Neiman Marcus employee does.

Webster Dictionary defines reliability with words such as "dependable and trustworthy."

No matter how good you are, or how good your price is, it may all come down to whether or not your customers can rely on you. A few years ago I heard an advertising salesman of a small public relations firm tell his client that he could have his project finished with excellent quality, great speed, and at a low price, but the client could only have two of the three.

Today, the salesman would lose his client. Those options should be standards, and probably are the client's expectations. The only variable might be the price.

Be reliable. It can be your competitive edge.

Magic Hints

• Reliability is proving to your customers that they can count on you.

• Test your reliability by asking these questions: How easy are we to do business with? How desirable are we to do business with?

• Make sure your customers can reach you. When you are not in your office, make arrangements for callers to reach you or leave messages.

• Be flexible to accommodate special or urgent requests.

• Carry out every promise you make.

• Be accountable. Take responsibility.

"Remember that a man's name is, to him, the sweetest and most important sound in any language."

-- Dale Carnegie

CHAPTER 11

STROKE YOUR CUSTOMER

Each of the suggestions so far has dealt strictly on a business level.

The final of these five ways to create moments of magic goes beyond "strictly business," into the realm of the personal. This is called stroking the customer.

Everyone needs to be told they are important. People thrive on praise. We like to feel appreciated.

So, you can create a *moment of magic* with your customers when you respond to their basic human needs for recognition. Take an interest in your customers as people. Use their names in conversation. Have fun with them. Recognize significant occasions. And most importantly, *say thanks.*

Take an Interest In Your Customers as People

Most people have a life away from their work. They have families, friends and hobbies and they enjoy leisure activities.

Get to know your customers. In a 30-second telephone conversation, you may just chat about weather in your part of the country versus theirs. In a long-term client relationship, you may become close friends and socialize with your customer away from work.

Famous business man and author, Harvey Mackay, has a form he calls the "Mackay 66." This is a questionnaire that has questions ranging from the customer business needs to the name of a spouse.

Smart business people know that a business relationship also is a personal relationship. The people must get to know each other so they can begin to work well together.

That is why companies hold retreats for their staffs. That is why company social events like picnics and bowling leagues are beneficial. They build working relationships. They help us see each other not just behind the desk, but as people.

Lunch is a great way to get acquainted with your customer in a more relaxed way. Salespeople take clients to lunch. Bosses take employees to lunch.

As you get to know your customers, you will find out what is important to them; their children, a hobby, or a cause. You will learn about significant events such as births, marriages and graduations. You can share your congratulations at joyous occasions, and your sympathies at negative events.

Recognize the Customer By Name

What is the favorite word anyone likes to hear? Their name!

Selective use of the customer's name can add sparkle to your relationship. It reminds the customer you are talking directly to them, and not anyone else.

On the phone, it can be very helpful to intersperse periodic "Yes, Mr. Jones" statements. At Venture discount department stores, the checkout clerks read the customer's name off of the credit card or check and say,

"Thank you, Ms. Smith."

It is a pleasure to visit a fine hotel and be greeted by name every time you pass through the lobby.

When we stayed at the Watergate Hotel in Washington, D.C., the people at the front desk greeted us by saying, "Mr. and Mrs. Hyken, it's so great to have you here. Is this your first time at our hotel? You're going to love it. We have a special room just for the two of you."

Three hours later, we were ready for dinner. As we passed through the lobby, we were greeted again: "Good evening, Mr. and Mrs. Hyken. Have a great night out."

This is the difference between a company that teaches people to care, and a company who teach their people to be clerks.

Have Fun With Your Customers

You can build relationships by having fun with your customers.

Sales people take their customers to professional sports events. At Halloween, retailers allow their employees to work in costume. One grocery store lets customers vote for their favorite checker.

On Southwest Airlines, flight attendants frequently will do fun things in the air. Some have even been known to do magic tricks.

Sharing a good joke or story is a good way to have fun with your customers. Another way is to share picture or mementos of family events or vacations.

Recognize Significant Occasions

Businesses typically send Christmas cards to their customers. That's a good idea. It keeps the company name in front of the customer, and is a way of saying thanks.

Many bosses send individualized Christmas cards to

employees. That provides an opportunity to thank the employee for the year's efforts.

Why not take this a step further? Why not send a card for the customer's birthday? Or the anniversary of your doing business together?

Jim Rhode has designed a marketing program to help dentists build their practices. He calls it event marketing. His clients not only send Christmas cards to their customers, they also send birthday cards and Valentine's Day cards.

Everyone likes recognition on their birthday. No matter how gruff or indifferent an exterior one may project, everyone has a soft spot for their birthday. People may say they are too old and do not want to remember, but that is hogwash.

Not only does Jim recognize these types of events, he also has his dentists send out regular postcards to help educate customers about dental care, and help them overcome fears of going to the dentist. Peanuts characters (Charlie Brown, Snoopy, Lucy, etc.) on the cards help to humanize the cards and add a light touch.

Say Thanks

One word you can never say often enough is thanks.

Thank your customers for doing business with you. Thank them for their ideas and anything they may have shared with you. I always appreciate receiving thank-you cards.

A meeting planner I know, Jim Nagel, has a card with the words "thank you" written repeatedly on the front of it. On the inside, it says "A million thanks." I liked the card enough that I asked him if I could borrow the design and print my own supply. I went through my first thousand in just over a year!

I carry a stack of the cards wherever I go. After I am finished with a speech, I may write several notes on the airplane during the trip home.

A few years ago, one of my clients offered me a full-time job, paying a healthy six-figure salary. I asked why they offered me the job. They said it was because of the thank-you notes I wrote.

They said, "You've worked for us six or eight times over the last couple years, and every single time you get together with us, whether its for a speech or to take you to lunch, you always write these little thank-you notes. They're so nice, it makes us feel like you really care about us, and you really care about our business. You do little things above and beyond the call of duty. We had an employee Christmas party, and you came and did a magic show and didn't charge us. If you could teach this attitude to the rest of our employees, you would be a very effective leader."

"Thank-you" also can be said in a large-scale way. My financial planner holds an elegant holiday party every year for his clients. Some companies have large employee picnics and special events. Each year, on the last home game of the season, the St. Louis Cardinals baseball team holds "Fan Appreciation Day." Anyone who buys a reserved seat for that last game of the season receives a coupon good for a free ticket to any home game the next season.

Ringling Brothers said thanks in a big way during the circus' 100th anniversary. Any child born during the anniversary year, could receive a free ticket to the circus, good anytime during the child's lifetime.

There are some special ways to say thank you and recognize employees, volunteers and other special groups. Awards and mementos can be given to all who contribute to a special project. Annual luncheons or dinners can provide a group thank-you and recall the accomplishments of the past year. Dressing up for an elegant banquet meal makes people feel special.

Stroke the customer. My friend Dr. Larry Baker says, "The most abused customer is the sold customer." Don't take your customers for granted. Let them know they are important.

Magic Hints

- Everyone likes to be told they are important.

- Say thanks. Write thank-you notes. Say thanks in person.

- Make time to visit informally with your customers and get to know them as people.

- Recognize your customers by name.

- Do fun activities like sponsoring contests, dressing up in costume or sharing jokes and stories.

- Recognize significant occasions like Christmas, birthdays, business anniversaries and others.

"In the long run, no matter how good or successful you are or how clever or crafty, your business and its future are in the hands of the people you hire."

-- Akio Morita,
Co-founder, Sony

PART III
PUTTING MOMENTS OF MAGIC TO WORK

Study and practice the five steps it takes to make magic, along with the five ways to create *moments of magic*.

Once you have mastered these skills, you are ready to face the biggest challenge in customer service - the irate customer. Following are some suggestions on handling complaining customers.

Another step involved in putting to work the *moments of magic* concepts is getting support throughout the organization. Even the best customer service program will not work unless it is supported by top management and by all employees.

"There is only one boss - the customer. Customers can fire everybody in the company from the chairman on down, simply by spending their money somewhere else."

-- Sam Walton

CHAPTER 12

HANDLING THE COMPLAINING CUSTOMER

Without a doubt, one of the single most important moments of truth is when the customer complains. More than any other time, that is when we put our reputations on the line.

We can turn the complaining customer into our friend, or we can turn them into our enemies. Often, there is not much middle ground. A customer complaint represents a dramatic turning point in the relationship between the customer and a business or organization.

Keep this in mind: We *want* our customers to complain when they are not happy. We *want* them to expect good service from us. Phil Wexler, noted author and trainer, says, "We want our complaining customers to become demanding customers."

Why Handling Complaints Is Important

We often have heard such statements as, "I had to call ABC Company three times before they straightened out my problem," "I sat on hold for 10 minutes before someone answered," or "They kept trying to convince me it was my problem and would not take responsibility for what they screwed up."

If you have been treated that way, you are not going to be happy. And if you are not happy, you are going to tell your friends. The White House Office of Consumer Affairs commissioned the Technical Assistance Research Program to do a study of customer complaints. The study showed that for every complaint, the complainer will tell an average of 10 other people about the situation. A segment of complainers, 13 percent, will tell over 20 people. If people are upset, they will talk about it.

By leaving one person unhappy, you actually are creating negative publicity about your organization for at least 10 people. Maybe you can afford to lose one customer. But can you afford to lose ten customers?

Here is more food for thought: That same study determined that for every customer who complained, 25 more people have complaints but did not come forward. What does this mean? For every one person who complains to you, there are another 25 people complaining to their friends, their parents, their kids, their cousins, everybody. In other words, 96 percent of the people out there who have a complaint, are not talking to you.

No matter how loyal your customers are, you eventually will lose them if you do not service their complaints. Charlie Mudd tells a story he calls "The Wyle E. Coyote Syndrome" at his company's sales meetings. In the cartoon "Road Runner," Wyle E. Coyote constantly destroys himself with Acme products. Whether it is dynamite, a truck or a ball, the Acme product never works. The dynamite blows up in the coyote's face. The truck crashes into the mountain because of bad brakes. But he keeps going back to Acme company for these faulty products. Now one day, he is going to wise up and realize that Acme is not a good deal. He is going to go to another supplier.

The same thing will happen to your customers if you fail to service them. Unhappy customers may continue to do business with you for a while, but they will eventually stop and take their business elsewhere.

The good news is that you can win over your customer with good service. If the customer complains, and you jump through hoops to take care of them, they will be your customers for life. And, they will tell 10 other people that you took care of them. They will be your best public relations.

Is the Customer Always Right?

Some people believe that the customer is always right. I disagree. My friend and colleague, Phil Wexler, says the customer is not always right, but they are always the customer. Sometimes customers can be irate, demanding and unreasonable. Just because we believe in serving the customer does not mean we must give in to every demand. If we have to operate by the rules and policies of our organizations, we may not be able to be as flexible as necessary. However, if the customer is not reasonable, we may not want to be flexible. We need to be helpful and work out a solution.

There are extreme examples of saying the customer is always right. The president of Nordstrom's department store brags about a customer who brought in a set of tires that were worn out and bald. The customer told the clerk the tires didn't perform well, and he demanded a refund (without a receipt, of course). The store gave him his money and took back the tires. There is one wrinkle: This store does not sell tires! It doesn't even have an automotive department! The Nordstrom's example shows how far they will go to make a customer happy. But is it reasonable?

Here is an alternative strategy, that might have served the interests of both the store and the customer. First, explain to the customer that the store does not sell tires and never has. Then, help the customer find a store that does sell tires, perhaps the brand that he has the problem with, or maybe even the store where the tires were originally purchased. That would have helped the customer without incurring an unjustified expense for the company, while leading the customer to a place that really can help him.

When the customer is wrong, we should attempt to educate them. Explain the situation without being offensive. Help them understand and come up with a reasonable solution.

The Three Responses

There are three ways of responding to customers; defensive, aggressive, and helpful.

When presented with a complaint, our instinctive response is to defend ourselves. If your spouse asks you why you were late, you may defend why you were late. This defensive response is similar to how some people respond when confronted by a customer. Defensiveness is *not* the best approach to handling customers, but is an approach people use over and over.

When people become defensive, they "backpedal" and make excuses. They rationalize their mistakes or other people's mistakes. They do not want their company to look like the bad guy. In essence, they are saying, "We're not wrong. You're wrong."

The defensive posture is rigid. It limits itself to just explaining to the customer why things were done a certain way. "This is our policy. We do not provide delivery outside of a three-mile radius. I am sorry, the salesman told you something we cannot do."

A variation of defensive behavior is aggressiveness. This posture attempts to change the customer's mind. "There is nothing wrong with this car. All of our engines make that clanking noise."

The customer may not always be right, but he deserves to be listened to.

There is a hotel I regularly use for seminars. My seminar normally starts at 8:00 a.m., with coffee service beginning at 7:45 a.m. For one particular seminar, we moved back the starting time a half hour to accommodate the hotel's request. They would need the room for an evening function, and it would help them for us to be out at 5 p.m. instead of 5:30 p.m., our usual ending time.

That morning, I arrived at 7:00 a.m. The contract for the meeting said coffee would be brought out by 7:15, with the seminar to start at 7:30. The time came, and there was no coffee. I found a catering employee, and asked where my coffee was. I was told no, this can not be done. The paperwork for catering said 7:45 coffee, 8:00 seminar, the usual schedule. Someone at the hotel had not changed the paperwork.

The employee insisted there was nothing he could do. He had to follow what was on his paperwork. We insisted that he follow our contract. When he refused, I said I would get the coffee myself. He said no, and it became a confrontation.

Aggressiveness Becomes Offensive

Another *moment of misery* came from a certain restaurant where I had decided to take my mother to lunch. After a short wait, we were seated. A few minutes later, the hostess came over and said, "You can't have this table."

I said, "My mother and I have already sat down. We are here."

She replied, "I didn't realize it, but the owner is here. He made a reservation for this table."

This restaurant did not accept reservations. I asked why couldn't the owner sit at another table. Finally, the owner himself came over and asked us to move. I was infuriated at being treated this way, especially with my mother as my guest. But I did not want to make a scene and embarrass her either. So, I complied with his request and silently vowed never to return to that restaurant again.

My vow lasted until a friend persuaded me to make another visit to that restaurant. Unfortunately, my second visit was worse than the first.

My friend ordered a chicken sandwich. The first half of the sandwich was fine. It had big chunks of chicken and he was pleased. But as he finished the sandwich, he noticed something in the chicken that did not taste right.

When the waitress asked how the meal was, my friend said it was fine although there was something wrong with a few chunks of chicken in the second half of the sandwich. He said he was just passing this on for information, since he already had finished the meal.

About two minutes later, the same owner, who evicted my mother and me from our table during the earlier visit, came to our table. The owner asked what was wrong with the chicken, and my friend explained.

The owner responded, "There's nothing wrong with our chicken. I made that chicken myself." My friend reiterated that something was wrong, although he was not asking for anything since he had finished the meal. However, the owner made it a confrontation. I left more disgusted with this restaurant.

However, another friend prevailed on me, and we gave this restaurant one more try. This day, the special was a half club sandwich and soup. I asked the server what was on the sandwich and was told it had bacon, lettuce, tomato, ham, cheese and mayonnaise. I asked if they could hold the mayonnaise.

"Well, I don't know," the server said. A few minutes later the owner walked over. You would think he knew me by now!

He said, "I understand we have a problem."

I said, "We do? I didn't think this was a problem."

"I understand you want your sandwich without mayonnaise."

"Yes, I do not want mayonnaise."

"This sandwich comes with mayonnaise."

"Just tell the chef to leave it off."

"But it is a half sandwich."

I said, "So what?"

He said, "What would we do with the other half of the sandwich?"

This manager was inflexible and offensive. We got up and left. Next time, no matter how persuasive my friends are, I will never go back to that restaurant.

Create an Empathetic Mood - Be Helpful

When the customer brings you a problem, you want them to know you are concerned and want to solve it.

Showing concern starts by listening. Studies have shown that 85 percent of communication is listening. The customer has contacted you because he or she has a problem, a need. They want to present it and get resolution.

Effective listening is work. Jeff Slutsky writes about a technique he calls the "mirror principle." With the mirror principle, you respond with a portion of your customer's comment. The customer says, "My computer is broken. When I bought it, I was told it would have a one-year warranty on all parts and labor." You say, "On all parts and labor?" And the customer says, "Yes, on parts and labor..." This lets the person know you are tuned into what they are saying.

When you use the mirror technique, it often leads the other person into further comments. In this case, the customer may have gone into a more detailed explanation. "When I was looking at these, I asked about warranty. The salesman said it had a full warranty."

Responding by asking questions is another technique that makes the customer feel like they are being heard. "You came here because you felt we could help you, right? Did you bring your copy of the maintenance agreement?"

Another effective listening technique is using the word "we." "It sounds like *we* have a misunderstanding here. What can *we* do to take care of this?"

Use the "That's Right!" Principle

A great technique for creating a positive atmosphere with your customer is the use of *"That's right!"* It brings you and the customer together. It places you and the customer on the same side of the issue. It puts you in a position of being *helpful* instead of *defensive*.

"That's right!" is taken from a card trick I learned as a child. In this card trick, the magician leads the audience to pick a certain card. In this example, we will attempt to get the person to pick the eight of hearts. Try this trick for yourself. You will need a friend to help you. Here's a sample of how it might go:

Magician: "How many cards are there in a deck of cards?"
Friend: "52."
Magician: "That's right. Now, I'm going to pick a card and I want you to guess it. I'm going to write it down.

First, in the deck there are red cards and black cards. Would you name either reds or blacks?"

Friend: "Reds."

Magician: "That's right. Of the reds, there are hearts and diamonds. Would you name either hearts or diamonds?"

Friend: "Hearts."

Magician: "That's right. Now of the hearts, you have number cards and you have picture cards. Would you name either numbers or pictures?"

Friend: "Numbers."

Magician: "That's right. Of the numbers, you have odds and evens. Would you name odd or even?"

Friend: "Even."

Magician: "That's right. Now of the even, you have the 2, 4, 6, 8 and 10 of hearts. Would you name three of those cards?"

Friend: "2, 4 and 8."

Magician: "That's right. Of the 2, 4 and 8, would you name two of those cards?"

Friend: "4 and 8."

Magician: "That's right. Of the 4 and 8, would you name one of those cards?"

Friend: "The 4."

Magician: "And that leaves the 8, doesn't it?"

Friend: "Yes."

Magician: "That's right. You just bought yourself the 8 of hearts!"

Look at the "script" carefully. Notice how the friend answered all of the questions correctly, except for the question:

"Of the 4 and 8, would you name one of these cards?"

It would have been perfect if our friend would have chosen eight, but he did not. He chose four. At this point we have a choice in how we respond. We can be pushy, defensive or helpful. Helpful means asking the question ...

"And that leaves the 8, doesn't it?"

Our friend agrees, and he is back on track.

What would have happened if in the beginning we asked our friend to name either reds or blacks, and our friend said blacks. We want them to say reds. What do we do? We ask the question ...

"That leaves reds, doesn't it?"

Our friend agrees, and he is back on track.

Try this trick on your friends. It's fun.

"That's right!" also is a very effective technique for disarming a hostile or irate customer. You use questions to ease confrontational situations.

When we truly know our business, we should be able to handle any confrontation with a customer, just by asking the right questions. If your business truly believes in delivering service, and the customer comes to you with a confrontation, start off by asking this very simple question:

"Isn't the reason you came to us to do business, because you wanted the quality service for which we have a good reputation?"

You say, "Yes." I say, *"That's right!"* It works wonderfully.

"That's Right!" at Work

An airline passenger walked up to the gate agent, very

upset that his flight to Los Angeles had just been canceled. The agent asked the passenger if he knew why the flight was canceled. The passenger said no.

The agent explained that the plane was found to have bad brakes. The agent did not make excuses, but gave an explanation. The agent asked the passenger, "You don't want to be on that airplane when it lands with bad brakes, do you?"

"No," said the passenger.

"That's right! You do want to get to Los Angeles on time or as close to on time, don't you?"

The passenger says "Yes." The agent asked where he wanted to go. The passenger said downtown Los Angeles. The agent noted that Los Angeles International is just one of four airports serving metropolitan Los Angeles to which the airline flew. He found a flight to Burbank that left 10 minutes sooner.

"By arriving 10 minutes early, you will make up the extra time it takes to get downtown," the agent said.

The customer was very thankful. A *moment of misery* had been turned into a *moment of magic*.

"That's right!" disarms the hostile customer. You don't say to the customer, "You're right, we're a lousy airline." That's not true. Instead, you educate the customer in a helpful way. The airline agent explained that the flight was canceled because the plane had bad brakes. Then, he asked the question, "Do you want to be on that plane with bad brakes?" The customer said, "No," and now they were thinking on the same wavelength.

The staff at a hotel used *"That's right!"* with me when my luggage was lost. They said to me, "We are glad you came to our hotel. We know that the reason you came here is because you know about our ability to take care of our customers. Isn't that true?"

I said, "Yes."

They said, "*That's right!* And we're not going to let you down." Then they analyzed the situation and solved it.

In this example, note how the employee brought up the positive points of the hotel. He reminded me of its reputation as a good hotel and why I wanted to stay there. This leads us to a very important point about customer service:

> **We are always selling ourselves and our organizations.**

Many people are uncomfortable with the idea of selling. But remember that selling yourself does not mean arm-twisting or manipulation. It simply means bringing up your positive points and keeping those in front of the customer. It can reinforce the customer's desire to do business with you, and prevent them from jumping to the competition.

"That's right!" and an Irate Customer

Here's another example.

The customer has just ordered 100,000 brochures from a printing company. The brochures arrived with smudges. A dialogue could go like this:

Customer: "I've just spent $40,000 to have you print my company brochure. We opened the boxes when they arrived, and found smudges all over the cover. We checked the proofs carefully all the way through. I don't understand how this happened. We have a mailing going out the 15th, and we can't use these. I am absolutely livid."

Service representative: "You came to us because you thought we were a good printer, didn't you?"

Customer: "Yes."

Service representative: "That's right. And we've disappointed you."

Customer: "Yes."

Service representative: "That's right. And we don't like to have disappointed customers. Now, let me ask you some questions to find out exactly what is going on. Can you show me a sample of one that is smudged?"

Customer: (Shows sample)

Service representative: "How many are like this?"

Customer: "We have checked about a fourth of the cartons, they're like this in about half."

Service representative: "Your mailing is going out the 15th. How many do you need?"

Customer: "Ten thousand."

Service representative: "If you can find enough good brochures to use for the mailing, go ahead and use those. In the meantime, we will reprint the job."

"*That's right!*" is part of a general way of thinking that allows us to listen to a complaint, rephrase it and let the customer know you hear it. In a sense, it is showing empathy for the customer.

What To Do If Nothing Works

Sometimes, you may try "*That's right!*" and other ways to listen and respond to the customer. You've shown empathy and sympathy. But the customer remains irate.

There is one more technique you can try. Ask them, "If you were me and I were you, and I was coming to you with this problem, what would you do? If you were Acme Industries, how would you handle this situation?" Ask the customer to be reasonable and realistic.

This causes the customer to recognize that his or her

demands are unreasonable and brings them back to reality.

Give Them a Reason To Come Back

You have faced the most irate customer. You have listened. You have built understanding with the help of *"That's right!"* You have come up with a solution.

The customer is satisfied. Everyone is happy. Is your job finished? Not quite.

There is one more thing you need to do to cement this customer relationship. Give them a reason to come back.

Solving the problem helps. But it does not guarantee that they will continue to do business with you. If you had a bad meal in a restaurant, wouldn't you think twice about going back, even if they replaced your meal or gave you a refund?

I am a regular customer of TGI Friday's, a national restaurant chain. They have consistent quality and service throughout. However, they are human, and on one occasion I received a bad meal. That gave me a chance to find out how well they resolve complaints.

I told the waitress my problem, and the manager took the meal off my bill. They also offered me my choice of another meal in its place. That is well and good. But the manager did something else important. He handed me his business card. On the back he wrote "Free appetizers and dessert for your entire party on your next visit."

Not only did he resolve the problem, but he gave me a reason to eat there again. He believes in TGI Friday's enough that he wants me to come back to prove they can do things right.

In a restaurant, that is very important. When you receive a bad meal, your confidence in the restaurant is broken. Replacing the meal or not charging you for it helps to ease the inconvenience. But it does not rebuild your confidence and trust. That can only come with another successful visit.

Business-To-Business Reason To Come Back

I nearly dropped my long-distance carrier due to an overcharge on my bills.

An independent telephone consultant had reviewed my long-distance service and found that I was not taking advantage of six-second incremental billing. Under this plan you are billed in six-second increments instead of one-minute increments. If you talk to someone for one minute and three seconds, you would have been charged two minutes under the old plan. Under six-second incremental billing, you are charged for one minute, six seconds. The consultant said I could save 15-20 percent off my bill by going to six-second incremental billing.

This program had been available from my carrier for two years, and I was not using it. I did not know about it. I called the company, and I was furious.

The person at the company said they send out all kinds of information about new programs in the monthly statements. This had been announced. I just didn't read it.

I wondered why they had not just switched me to six-second incremental billing automatically. They said that has to be the customer's decision. Various programs suit various kinds of customers.

What the company offered to do was to give me a 15 percent credit on every bill over the past two years. Rather than pay me cash, they said they would credit it against future long-distance bills. There was one condition. I had to stay with this carrier.

By now, I was disgusted with the company and was ready to change carriers. But if I wanted to get this credit, I would have to stay with them. Who could pass up a couple of month's free long-distance service?

I ended up staying with the carrier and taking the credit. They regained my trust. By setting up the credit the way they did, they gave me a reason to stay with them. They had another chance to show me how good they were.

A Tale of Two Hotels

I was staying at a very famous and expensive hotel in downtown Atlanta. The corporate rate was $195 a night. I arrived late at night. The lobby was beautiful and the people at the front desk were very nice. I thought I was in for a positive experience. I recognize and appreciate good service.

Unfortunately, once I stepped out of the elevator onto my floor, everything began to go wrong. Little things. The rug was worn. The wallpaper was torn. When I went to turn on the lights, the light switch fell out of the wall. I sat in the chair at the desk, and the leg was broken. I almost fell over.

I called the operator to request a wake-up call, because the alarm clock did not seem to work. The phone rang and rang for the operator. When someone answered, they put me on hold. Then, they were rude.

The next day, my office had sent a fax to me via the hotel's front desk. No one from the hotel brought it to the room or even called me to say it had arrived.

Then I asked to have the manager call me. He never called.

At check-out time, I asked to see the manager. I gave him a list of more than 20 problems I had experienced with the hotel's facilities and service.

The manager offered to take $100 off my room each night, about half the $195 rate. I accepted that offer, but I walked away without any of the problems being solved.

Since the manager could not solve the problems after the

fact, what was really missing was an incentive to get me to return. Giving me a credit was okay, but it was not a complete solution. They haven't redeemed themselves and shown me they can do the job right. The manager did not offer me a reason to come back.

Next, here is one hotel that did redeem itself.

My wife and I stayed at the Ambassador East Hotel on a weekend trip to Chicago. Overall, our experience was very positive.

I like to write on the comment cards they leave in the room and rate the service, especially when it is good service. In this case, everything was almost perfect. There was only one problem I noticed. The hotel had advertised turndown service, where they turn back your bed covers in the evening, freshen up the room and leave some type of evening refreshment, such as mints or cookies. There was even a flyer on the bed advertising this service.

But, when we returned to our room for the night, we had not received the advertised turndown service. This happened for two more nights. It was not a problem and not an inconvenience, but I did note it on the comment card, just to let them know. I was not complaining.

Several weeks later, I received a letter from the manager of the hotel saying how sorry they were. "A hotel like ours should not forget those things. The next time you are in this area, stay at our hotel. We will give you the first night free. By the way, we also have a new athletic club."

Nice move. The hotel used this as an opportunity to remind me about their amenities. They gave me a reason to come back. Since then, I have gone back, and more than a few times.

Magic Hints

- We *want* our customers to complain when they are not happy. We *want* them to be demanding of us.

- When a customer has a complaint, they will tell an average of ten other people.

- For every customer who complains, another 25 have the same problem but do not complain.

- No matter how loyal your customers are, they eventually will take their business elsewhere if you do not satisfy their complaints.

- The customer is *not* always right, but they are always the customer. When they make unreasonable demands, we should educate them.

- Three ways of responding to the customer are defensive, aggressive and helpful. Defensiveness is limited to explaining what was done and why. Aggressiveness attempts to change the customer's mind. Helpful response is centered on the customer's needs.

- Use effective listening skills to create an empathetic mood with the customer.

- *"That's right!"* is a useful technique to neutralize complaining customers.

- We need to use every contact with the customer as an opportunity to sell ourselves and the organizations we serve.

• Give the complaining customer a reason to come back and do business with you again. One example is to provide a free offer or discount on the customer's *next* visit. Solving the problem is just the first step. Now you must show the customer just how good you really are.

"Treat the employee the way you want the employee to treat the customer."

-- Steven R. Covey
Author, 7 Habits of Highly Effective
People

CHAPTER 13

BUILDING A TEAM SPIRIT OF SERVICE

If your company or organization consists of more than just you, then you need to work at building a spirit of teamwork and service. Everyone in the company needs to display a service-minded attitude.

Good service is an attitude that extends throughout a company. It is a friendly, cooperative, get-it-done attitude. You can feel the magic of this spirit sparkle among everyone you see.

In contrast, a bad attitude can permeate a company, too. It is like a black cloud. People shuffle around and seem not to care about what they are doing. In companies which push their people unrealistically, the attitude comes across in employees who are short-tempered with customers.

Attitude is important in *every* part of the company, not just the customer service department. The internal customer is the person inside the company whom you serve in your job. It may be a department to where you deliver reports, or the next person in the production process. It may be your boss, or the employees you supervise. It all comes down to this:

**No matter where you work or what you
do, you are in customer service.**

To illustrate the importance of internal service within a company, consider the case of a procurement department. Other people in the company come to this department to order their supplies. The people in the department move laboriously slow and give you a "whadayawant" attitude. Do you want to go back there for your supplies? Do you think about ordering your supplies outside on your own? Does the way these people represent your company make you feel proud?

Now, consider the effect of a procurement department staffed with people who are pleasant and efficient. How does that make you feel about your company? Are you more inclined to want to give good service also? When people greet you cheerfully and perform responsively, that inspires you to a higher standard. If you work in a company with upbeat people, you will tend to be more upbeat. You will feel more pride in the company.

Much has been said and written about employee motivation. Programs and buzz words have come and gone.

For some, employee motivation is nothing more than posters and slogans. Many times, these type of gimmicks are just superficial band-aids. For the person on the assembly line, posters and slogans about quality are meaningless if the plant is still dirty, supervisors treat employees poorly, and the company emphasizes production above quality.

Service and quality are an attitude. They start at the top echelons of the company. They are carried out in everything the company does.

Here are four steps your organization can take to build a winning spirit:

- Create an attitude of service.
- Start this attitude at the top and filter it down.
- Understand employees as customers.
- Give praise.

Create an Attitude of Service

Like any important commitment, becoming a service-minded company starts with a decision. Yes, we are going to make service our first priority.

This dedication to service should be as fundamental as a company's mission statement. Some companies have incorporated service into their statements of corporate philosophy.

Kinko's, a relatively young company, has built its business on a philosophy of customer service.

The Kinko's Philosophy

Our primary objective is to take care of our customer. We are proud of our ability to serve him or her in a timely and helpful manner, and to provide high quality at a reasonable price. We develop long-term relationships that promote mutual growth and prosperity. We value creativity, productivity, and loyalty, and we encourage independent thinking and teamwork.

We openly communicate our accomplishments and mistakes so we can learn from each other. We consider ourselves part of the Kinko's family. We trust and care for each other, and treat everyone with respect. We strive to live balanced lives in work, love, and play. We are confident of our future and point with pride to the way we run our business, care for our environment, and treat each other.

Johnson & Johnson's credo helped guide its effective

handling of the Tylenol crisis. When you read this credo, you know that if you are Johnson & Johnson, you cannot skimp or take the easy way out when it comes to the customer.

Johnson & Johnson's Credo

We believe our first responsibility is to the doctors, nurses and patients, to mothers and fathers and all others who use our products and services. In meeting their needs everything we do must be of high quality. We must constantly strive to reduce our costs in order to maintain reasonable prices. Customers' orders must be serviced promptly and accurately. Our suppliers and distributors must have an opportunity to make a fair profit.

We are responsible to our employees, the men and women who work with us throughout the world. Everyone must be considered as an individual. We must respect their dignity and recognize their merit. They must have a sense of security in their jobs. Compensation must be fair and adequate. We must be mindful of ways to help our employees fulfill their family responsibilities. Employees must feel free to make suggestions and complaints. There must be equal opportunity for employment, development and advancement for those qualified. We must provide competent management, and their actions must be just and ethical.

We are responsible to the communities in which we live and work and to the world community as well. We must be good citizens - support good works and charities and bear our fair share of taxes. We must encourage civic improvements and better health and education. We must maintain in good order the property we are privileged to use, protecting the environment and natural resources.

Our final responsibility is to our stockholders. Business

must make a sound profit. We must experiment with new ideas. Research must be carried on, innovative programs developed and mistakes paid for. New equipment must be purchased, new facilities provided and new products launched. Reserves must be created to provide for adverse times. When we operate according to these principles, the stockholders should realize a fair return.

Ritz-Carlton's credo exemplifies the hotel's dedication to service. It is simple and direct.

The Ritz-Carlton Credo

The Ritz-Carlton Hotel is a place where the genuine care and comfort of our guests is our highest mission.

We pledge to provide the finest personal service and facilities for our guests who will always enjoy a warm, relaxed yet refined ambience.

The Ritz-Carlton experience enlivens the senses, instills well-being, and fulfills even the unexpressed wishes and needs of our guests.

Wetterau Incorporated is a successful wholesaler to independent grocery stores. Its creed indicates a company dedicated to high principles of service:

The Wetterau Creed

We believe that people should be treated as we would like to be treated, and that this applies to the welfare of our employees and their families, to our suppliers and all with whom we do business.

We believe that successful independent business is the backbone of our country, that our success is closely related to the success of our retail customers, and that only by working together can the ultimate success of both partners be assured.

We, therefore, dedicate ourselves to work for our mutual success and we pledge our best efforts always toward the attainment of our common goal.

A corporate philosophy or credo should be honored and revered. It should be displayed prominently in company offices. It should be printed in the annual report and the profile brochure. It should be part of the company tradition.

Employees should take the credo seriously. They will do so only if the company also takes the credo seriously, by publishing it, displaying it, and living by it.

Other statements besides corporate credos can be useful in focusing employees on service. The following statements from Lexus are not corporate philosophies or credos, but are good motivators. These messages are printed on business-card-size stock and are laminated. Employees are encouraged to carry these cards.

The Lexus Covenant

Lexus will enter the most competitive, prestigious automobile race in the world. Over 50 years of Toyota automotive experience has culminated in the creation of Lexus cars. They will be the finest cars ever built.

Lexus will win the race because: Lexus will do it right from the start. Lexus will have the finest dealer network in the industry. Lexus will treat each customer as we would a guest in our home.

If you think you can't, you won't... If you think you can, you will! We can, we will.

As a Lexus Representative I:

L - *Listen to the concerns of the Customer*
E - *Empathize with the Customer's feelings*
X - *Examine options for a solution*
U - *Understand Customer's worth to Lexus*
S - *Sincerely want to help*

C - *Communicate the best solution*
A - *Answer the Customer's questions*
R - *Respond to the Customer's needs*
E - *Exceed the Customer's needs*
S - *"Satisfy the Customer"*

Start This Attitude at the Top

Top management must set the example for service. If top management does not practice good service, their words and credos lose all credibility.

Good service is practiced in two ways:
1. By the way executives treat customers and the modeling they provide,
2. By the way executives treat employees, in that employees will not treat customers much different from the way they are treated.

Employees want to feel valued and appreciated for what they do. When they are charged up and their morale is good, they will produce more.

Upper management should think of itself not as the boss, but as a coach or mentor. A definition of leadership is "getting things done through other people." Good executives don't manage, they lead. They empower people to carry out the responsibilities they are capable of.

Tom Peters advocates a concept he calls MBWA - Management By Walking Around. Executives should get out of the office and onto the floor. They should visit informally with employees on the job. They should create an atmosphere of mutual respect, not of master and slave. Find out what is going on. Do employees seem happy? Are problems being brought up?

MBWA is a good idea because it keeps management visible. If top management visits the plant only when there are problems, then people will be intimidated when management appears. MBWA disarms uncomfortable feelings. It breaks down barriers and helps to build a team concept. People are not afraid when they see the boss, because they are used to the boss being around.

There are other ways to bridge the management-employee gap. One company periodically places its executives in entry-level or line jobs in other departments. The executive is to be treated as a beginner in the job.

This has important benefits. First, it makes the executives sensitive to the needs of other departments. When they make demands of that department, they have a better understanding of how the department performs its work. Second, it makes them more sensitive to lower-level employees. It breaks down barriers of status and rank. Finally, it is a source of new ideas. Frequently, executives came back with new ideas for both their own department and the department they were visiting. By changing their perspective, they get a fresh view of the company. For example, a sales executive could go into production and ask, "Why are we doing things this way?" It stimulates everyone's thinking from top to bottom.

Understand Employees as Your Customers

In a previous chapter we discussed ways to understand your customers. The same techniques apply for employees. Remember this one-line poem:

Think like the buyer, not like the supplier.

Maintain Lines of Communication

Make sure employees can come to you with problems. Make yourself accessible. Have an "open door" policy. Talk informally with employees and supervisors. Conduct your own informal polls to keep the pulse of employee opinion. Formal surveys are also useful. These should be done professionally and with strict regard for confidentiality. If employees feel their comments can be traced back to them, they may not be honest about problems.

Treat Employees As Individuals

No two people are alike. Each of us has different needs we seek to fulfill.

It is helpful in the workplace to be aware of personality differences. Myers-Briggs is a popular system for personality profiling. It groups people in four areas: introvert vs. extravert, intuitive vs. sensing, feeling vs. thinking, and perceptive vs. judgmental.

The classic example of a wife who says, "My husband doesn't appreciate me, he never says anything nice to me," often is really due to personality differences in feeling versus thinking. The wife is feeling-oriented, and needs more strokes like, "You are a nice person, you are fun to be around, you really look nice." The husband is thinking-oriented and does not have that need to the same degree. He says, "Why does she always want to hear this? Doesn't she know I love her?"

Turning to the other Myers-Briggs types, an introvert (I) has less of a need to be around people than an extravert (E). You are more likely to find introverts in computer programming, and extraverts in sales.

Intuitive (N) people are idea people. They ask, "What if?" Sensing (S) people deal with facts in front of them. Accountants are more likely to be sensing, while advertising is a good place to look for intuitives.

Judgmental (J) people like time structure and closure. If a project needs to be done by Friday, it will be done. Perceptive (P) people prefer to leave things more open-ended. They say, "Let's wait and see." A "J" office will be neat and orderly, with the desk clear. A "P" office will be cluttered with a wide range of projects and papers, all of which have some reason for being there.

It is important to remember that there is no right or wrong to any of these types. Each has its advantages. Perception and intuition help us to be more creative and consider more possibilities. Sensing and judgment help us deal with the facts before us and take specific action.

Each of us has all eight characteristics to some degree. It is most healthy for us to develop our capabilities in all eight areas. If we fall extremely to one end in any of the axes, we may need to work to relate to people at the opposite end.

In companies where Myers-Briggs or other personality typing exercises have been conducted, it is an eye-opening experience. People gain new understanding and appreciation of other employees. They learn why Mr. Smith always drives Mrs. Jones crazy. He is a "Perceptive" and she is a "Judgmental." By recognizing these characteristics, we can appreciate our differences. We can see the value of different approaches.

Understanding personality types works both ways in the employer-employee relationship. If you are giving a presentation to a detail-minded executive, you need to be prepared with facts and examples. Maybe you should give a formal presentation with slides. For another executive, we may operate more informally. You might give a report over a cup of coffee. The executive says, "Just give me the big picture." He relies on others for the details. Again, neither way is right or wrong.

Get Employees Involved

To build team spirit in your organization, you must get people to think beyond their own jobs. They must be aware of the entire organization and its mission.

Encourage them to go to work for the company, not just a paycheck. Remember the function of a business? To get and keep customers. Everyone has a stake in that.

A home remodeling company was having problems in its telemarketing department. Turnover was high, and morale was low. Money was not a problem, they were well paid. Was it burnout?

I asked the company president how he kept his people motivated. He said they have pep talks. I asked if the telemarketers believe in the product they sell. He was not sure. It was obvious he believed in his product, but the important question was, did the telemarketing department believe in it?

These types of telemarketers have an inherently unpleasant job. They call people in the middle of dinner, interrupt them, and ask them if they need siding, windows or a new roof. Comedian Jerry Seinfeld has a routine on telemarketers. When answering a call from a solicitor, he asks for the solicitors' home number so he can call him back later. When the solicitor refuses to give a home number, he says, "What, you don't want to get calls at home? Well, now you know how it feels." He hangs up. We may not like to receive solicitor calls, and for telemarketers, it may not be fun to give the calls either.

I proposed an idea to the company president. Once the

telemarketer has produced a lead, it is turned over to the sales representative. The telemarketer has no further contact with the customer, although one in three leads turn into a sale. I suggested that after the sale is completed, the company have their telemarketers call the customers they produced. They would ask the customers if they are satisfied. Previously, the sales representative had made this follow-up call. This way, the telemarketer would have a second contact with the customer, and could hear first-hand about how good the company's products are.

The idea worked. Turnover among the top telemarketers dropped sharply. The reason it worked was that the telemarketers got to hear first-hand feedback from the customer. The feedback was good, and the telemarketers had a good feeling about what they were doing.

Give Praise

Surveys show again and again that a paycheck is just one of many reasons that employees work. Self-fulfillment and a sense of self worth, also are strong reasons.

Some people quit jobs which pay well but are not personally satisfying.

Therefore, it is important for companies to recognize their employees and let them know they are appreciated. Recognition may be done formally and informally.

Formal Recognition

Award and incentive programs are ways to provide formal recognition. If you produce beyond a certain level, you receive a bonus or what some companies call a "President's Award."

Large sales organizations typically have strong incentive programs. Top sellers might receive free trips to Hawaii or Jamaica. Coupled with this is peer recognition.

The entire sales force knows that Bill, Sally, Sam and Susan won the trip and the award. Sales awards often are given at annual meetings of the sales force.

Promotion and pay raises are another form of recognition. Smart companies have career tracks and find ways to develop good people.

Most companies also give awards for longevity of service.

Informal Recognition

Just as important as formal programs, are the informal pats on the back. When the company president sees you in the hall and congratulates you on a great job, that makes you feel good.

One company has an employee appreciation week. They provide free donuts for everyone in the office. They give out roses to employees. There is a luncheon one day.

Holiday parties and other dinner/socials give informal recognition. Employees are treated to a nice meal and get a chance to dress up. The president speaks and thanks everyone for their work during the year. Perhaps there is some humor, such as a roast or skit on the company.

Informal praise can be summed up by this poem by Helen Lowrie Marshall, from *The Gift of Wonder*:

I spoke a word of praise today,
One I had no need to say.
I spoke a word of praise to one
Commending some small service done,
And in return, to my surprise,
I reaped rewards of mountain size;
For such a look of pleasure shone
Upon his face -- I'll never own
A gift more beautiful to see

Than that swift smile he gave to me.
I spoke one little word of praise
And sunshine fell on both our ways.

Build teamwork with your employees. Set an example of good service, both in how you treat the customer and how you treat the employee. Treat the employee the way you would want the employee to treat the customer. Understand the employee's needs, get employees involved and respect individual differences. Practice "Management By Walking Around," and keep close to the pulse of your organization. Praise work well done, and let everyone know they are important.

Remember that every employee has customers, no matter what their job. It may be one department or the entire company, or it may be the outside customer.

When you create *moments of magic* with your internal customers, that will naturally spread to *moments of magic* for the outside customer.

Magic Hints

- Good service is an attitude that extends throughout a company.

- Everyone is involved with customer service, even if they are not dealing directly with the outside customer.

- Corporate philosophies and creeds give a written commitment to service, to which everyone can refer.

- Top management must set the example for good service.

- Maintain lines of communication with employees.

- Treat employees as individuals.

- Get employees involved in your business by exposing them to other parts of the operation.

- Give praise through formal and informal programs.

"Service is a position of power, even of love. I can't understand why more intelligent people don't take it as a career. Learn to do it well."

-- *John Steinbeck*

CHAPTER 14

CONCLUSION

Good customer service is essential to survival in the 1990s. That goes for organizations and for their individual employees.

Businesses face an increasingly sophisticated marketplace. Consumers have more information available to them than ever before. There is a wealth of advice in the media on how to shop for everything from refrigerators to mutual funds to nursing homes. People know what questions to ask, and are less likely to buy with little knowledge.

Customers have learned to expect more. The influx of foreign-made goods in the United States has raised consumer expectations of quality. General Motors, once a dinosaur of customer-mindedness, now offers programs like free emergency road service on Pontiacs and a 30-day free exchange guarantee on Oldsmobiles. Their luxury division, Cadillac, is a recipient of the Malcolm Baldridge Quality award.

With these higher expectations, consumers are doing more shopping around. Businesses now request annual bids on printing, insurance and other contracts which once went to the same vendors year after year. Loyalty to vendors is not the same as it has been in the past. What this means for business is you cannot rest on your laurels. You have to go out every day and prove yourself. You have to keep improving to stay ahead of the competition. A critical ingredient of success is excellent customer service. Within their organizations, individual employees face a similar situation.

More is expected of employees today. In recent years, business has shrunk employment ranks through downsizing. Each job is examined for its contribution to the organization and the bottom line. Facing a competitive world marketplace, companies are pressured to keep their costs as low as possible. Employers can no longer afford to carry excess positions.

What does this mean for the employee? One must produce, or face the possibility of their job being eliminated. To keep yourself in good standing within your organization you must pay constant attention to serving your internal customers. Those customers are other employees, clients and suppliers with whom you work.

Internal customers must be served with every bit of the speed, reliability and quality that we would give to the outside customer.

So, if you want to stay on top, heed these words:

Pay attention to your customers (internal & external).

Customer Service - Key To Success

In the 1990s it will be essential to give good service to the outside customer and the inside customer.

While I like to describe a moment of good service as a *moment of magic*, there is nothing mysterious about how to create magic with your customers.

Anyone can become a maker of magic in customer service. Good service is nothing more than good business practice. Anyone can learn the tools and skills needed to give good service.

To recap, these include five steps to turn yourself into a maker of magic: Make a good first impression; know your business; be informed and know a little about many things; be enthusiastic; and understand your customer. In addition, there are five ways to create magic: Provide quality at every turn; respond quickly; solve problems; be reliable; and stroke the customer.

Most importantly, you must commit yourself to raise your level of customer service. Study each of these ten steps and practice them. Study the additional readings listed in the Appendix.

Good service starts with an attitude that your customers are important, and you make it a priority to take care of them. You care about what you do and it shows. You put yourself in their shoes, and *think like the buyer, not like the supplier*.

Remember that every contact with the customer is a moment of truth. You can turn it into a *moment of magic*.

You are always selling yourself and your organization. Be informed. Talk positively. Recognize your and your organization's attributes, and highlight them. Let people know what you do well. No one else can represent you better than you.

At the same time, be empathetic to the customer. Listen to what they say. Think about ways their needs can be better served.

The *moments of magic* concepts work in your personal life, too.

Treat your spouse, children, family and friends as you

would treat a customer. The same elements of good customer service apply to relationships.

Respond to their needs and requests on a timely basis. Follow through on your promises and be accountable. Stroke your family and say thanks. Think about their needs and how they might be met. Read and study on issues of concern to family and friends.

All of these elements go to making good personal relationships. Of course, they go to making good business relationships, too.

Monitor Your Progress

Once you have introduced yourself to the concepts of *moments of magic*, it's time to put them to work.

You can use the following checklist to review your progress, and see how good of a maker of magic you have become. Review the checklist periodically to make sure you are not slipping into any bad habits.

Moments of Magic Checklist

✓ How do you answer the telephone? Is your greeting pleasant and inviting to the customer?

✓ When you meet customers, do you dress appropriately?

✓ What periodicals, books, etc. do you read about your business?

✓ When was the last seminar you attended? Do you participate in your professional or trade association?

✓ Can you name and describe the major events and issues occurring in your community, nation and the world today?

✓ Do you project an enthusiastic attitude? Do you show other people that you care about your work?

✓ Do you view work situations with a positive, "We will solve this" attitude?

✓ Do you ask your customers for their opinions?

✓ Do you think about ways that your customers' needs could be better met?

✓ Are you doing a thorough job, so your work does not have to be redone?

✓ Is your correspondence clean, and does it meet or exceed current standards?

✓ Are you up to date in responding to customer requests?

✓ Do you take action to resolve customer problems that are brought to you?

✓ When you make a promise, do you follow through?

✓ How accessible are you to people who wish to reach you in person or by phone?

✓ Do you say "thank you" to your customers?

✓ When you handle a customer complaint, do you provide something that gives the customer a reason to want to do business with you again?

✓ Does your organization communicate an attitude of

service?

✓ Does your top management set the example for good customer service?

Service is Everyone's Business

No matter who you are or what you do, you have customer relationships. You have people to whom you provide a product or service, in your business life as well as your personal life.

A secret of successful people is that they give good, timely service. They have built a reputation. With the help of *moments of magic*, you can learn how to give good service, too.

By learning the secrets of good customer service, you can turn ordinary moments of truth into...

Moments of Magic!!!

Appendix

Recommended Reading

Albrecht, Karl and Bradford, Lawrence J.; *The Service Advantage*; Dow Jones-Irwin

Albrecht, Karl; *At America's Service*; Dow Jones-Irwin

Albrecht, Karl; *The Only Thing that Matters*; Harper Business, a division of HarperCollins Publishers, Inc.; 10 East 53rd Street, New York, N.Y. 10022.

Albrecht, Karl and Zemke, Ron; *Service America!*; Dow Jones-Irwin

Alessandra, Tony Ph.D., Wexler, Phil and Barrera, Rick; *Non-Manipulative Selling*; Prentice Hall Press; Gulf & Western Building; One Gulf & Western Plaza, New York, NY 10023

Blanchard, Kenneth, Ph.D.; *The One Minute Manager*; The Berkley Publishing Group; 200 Madison Ave, New York, NY 10016

Carlzon, Jan; *Moments of Truth*; Harper & Row, Publishers, Inc.; 10 East 53rd Street, New York, NY 10022

Communication Briefings; 700 Black Horse Pike, Suite 110, Blackwood, NJ 08012

Davidow, Hilliam H. and Uttal Bro; *Total Customer Service*; Harper & Row, Publishers, Inc.; 10 East 53rd Street, New York, NY 10022

Fromm, Bill; *The 10 Commandments of Business and How to Break Them*; The Berkly Publishing Group; 200 Madison Avenue, New York, NY 10016

Parker, Glenn M.; *Team Players and Teamwork*; Jossey-Bass, Inc., 350 Sansom St., San Francisco, CA 94104

Hanan, Mack and Karp, Peter; *Customer Satisfaction*; AMACOM, a division of American Management Association; 135 West 50th Street, New York, NY 10020

Kriegel, Robert J. and Patler Louis; *If it Ain't Broke Break It*; Warner Books, Inc.; 1271 Avenue of the Americas, New York, NY 10020

LeBoeuf, Michael, Ph.D.; *How to Win Customers and Keep Them for Life*; G.P. Putnam's Sons; 200 Madison Avenue, New York, NY 10016

Mackay, Harvey; *Beware the Naked Man Who Offers You His Shirt*; William Morrow and Company, Inc.; 105 Madison Ave., NewYork, NY 10016

Mackay, Harvey; *Swim with the Sharks Without Being Eaten Alive*; William Morrow and Company, Inc.; 105 Madison Ave, NewYork, NY 10016

McKenna, Regis; *Relationship Marketing*; Addison-Wesley Publishing Co.; Route 128, Reading, MA 01867

Metejka, Ken; *Why this Horse Won't Drink*; AMACOM, a division of American Management Association; 135 West Street, New York, NY 10020

Peters, Tom and Austin, Nancy; *A Passion for Excellence*; Random House, Inc.; 201 East 50th Street, New York, NY 10022

Peters, Thomas and Waterman Jr.; *In Search of Excellence*; Harper & Row, Publishers, Inc.; 10 East 53rd Street, New York, N.Y. 10022.

Reilly, Tom; *Value Added Selling Techniques*; Motivatin Press; 1302 Clarkson Clayton Center, Suite 205, Ellisville, MO 63011

Sewell, Carl and Brown, Paul; *Customers for Life*; Doubleday a division of Bantam Doubleday Dell Publishing Group, Inc.; 666 Fifth Ave, New York, NY 10103

Walther, George R.; *Power Talking*; G.P. Putnam's Sons; 200 Madison Avenue, New York, NY 10016

Wexler, Phillip, Adams, W.A. (Bill) and Bohn, Emil, Ph.D; *The Quest for Service Quality*; Maxcomm Associates, Inc.; 1333 East 9400 South, Suite 270, Sandy, Utah 84093

Wexler, Phil and Shapiro, Steve; *The Art of Professional Serving*; Resource Publishing Group; 1742 Garnet Ave., Suite 125; San Diego, CA 92109

Winninger, Tom; *Price Wars: How To Win The Battle For Your Customer*; St. Thomas Press; 4510 West 77th St., Suite 210, Minneapolis, MN 55435

Yager, Jan; *Business Protocal*; John Wiley & Sons, Inc.; 605 Third Avenue, New York, NY 10158

Zemke, Ron and Schaaf, Dick; *The Service Edge*; Lakewood Publications; 50 South Ninth St., Minneapolis, MN 55402

About the Author

Shep Hyken, CSP is a professional speaker who has been entertaining audiences with his unique presentation style for over 25 years. He has been hailed as one of the top entertainer/magicians working the corporate field. In 1983 he made the transition from entertainer to speaker, blending his entertaining talents with topics on service. His presentations combine information and entertainment (humor and magic) to create exciting programs.

Shep's most popular programs focus on customer loyalty, customer service, customer relations and internal service. He also has a motivational speech titled *You Are the Magic!* and a unique program called *Focus On the Customer - Live!*

As a speaker and consultant, Shep Hyken has worked with hundreds of companies and associations ranging from "Fortune 500" size corporations to smaller companies with less than 50 employees. Some of his clients include American Airlines, Anheuser-Busch, ARA, AT&T, Citicorp, Ford, General Electric, General Motors, Hertz, Holiday Inn, Hyatt Hotels, IBM, Johnson & Johnson, Kraft, Marriott, Million Dollar Round Table, Monsanto, Shell Oil, Southwestern Bell, Standard Oil, TWA, Winn Dixie, Young Presidents Organization and many more.

* CSP (Certified Speaking Professional) is a designation awarded by the National Speakers Association to individuals for certain achievements and education in the speaking profession.

Shep Hyken, CSP
Shepard Presentations
(314) 692-2200
Email: shep@hyken.com
www.hyken.com